HER SPACE, HER PLACE

A Geography of Women

Mary Ellen Mazey
Department of Geography
Wright State University
Dayton, Ohio

David R. Lee
Department of Geography
Florida Atlantic University
Boca Raton

RESOURCE PUBLICATIONS
IN GEOGRAPHY

HQ
1206
.M364
1983

Library of Congress Card Number 83-22289
ISBN 0-89291-172-7

Library of Congress Cataloging in Publication Data

Mazey, Mary Ellen, 1949-
  Her space, her place.

  (Resource publications in geography)
  Bibliography: p.
  1. Women. 2. Women — United States. 3. Women's studies.
4. Anthropo-geography. 5. Human ecology.
I. Lee, David R., 1937-   . II. Title, III. Series.
HQ1206.M364   1983   305.4   83-22289
ISBN 0-89291-172-7

Publication Supported by the A.A.G.

Graphic Design by CGK

Printed by Commercial Printing Inc.
State College, Pennsylvania

Foreword

It is perhaps ironic that a discipline that has prided itself on an ability to observe, to record, and to analyze the world around us could remain largely ignorant of significant spatial patterns, processes, and problems. Geographers have addressed, with rigor and dedication, problems of Third World development, appropriate technology, natural resource conservation, racial and social inequities, urban decay, and a vast number of other valuable issues. Why, then, have we been comparatively blind to geographical problems and ideas concerning women? Answers, Mazey and Lee suggest, may be found in the spatial distribution and dispersion of women, as well in the seemingly ubiquitous masculine bias of our science.

In this unabashedly feminist book, Mazey and Lee use traditional geographical themes — spatial distribution, spatial analysis, diffusion, and the cultural landscape, among others — to suggest new directions in the study of the geography of women. There are major opportunities and obligations for human geographers to deal with feminist issues. This book offers an important first step in that direction.

Resource Publications in Geography are sponsored by the Association of American Geographers, a professional organization whose purpose is to advance studies in geography and to encourage the application of geographic research in education, government, and business. This series traces its origins to the Association's Commission on College Geography, whose *Resource Papers* were launched in 1968. Eventually 28 papers were published under sponsorship of the Commission through 1974 with the assistance of the National Science Foundation. Continued NSF support after completion of the Commission's work permitted the *Resource Papers for College Geography* to meet the original series goals for an additional four years and sixteen volumes:

> The Resource Papers have been developed as expository documents for the use of both the student and the instructor. They are experimental in that they are designed to supplement existing texts and to fill a gap between significant research in American geography and readily accessible materials. The papers are concerned with important concepts or topics in modern geography and focus on one of three general themes: geographic theory; policy implications; or contemporary social relevance. They are designed to supplement a variety of undergraduate college geography courses at the introductory and advanced level.

The popularity and usefulness of the two series suggested the importance of their continuation after 1978 once a self-supporting basis for their publication had been established.

For the *Resource Publications,* the original goals remain paramount. However, they have been broadened to include the continuing education of professional geographers as well as communication with the public on contemporary issues of geographic relevance. This monograph was developed, printed and distributed under the auspices of the Associaton, whose members served in advisory and review roles during its preparation. The ideas presented, however, are the authors' and do not imply AAG endorsement.

The editor and advisory board hope that this volume will be a challenge to conventional geographical wisdom, not so much in our theory and method, but in our ability to comprehend the world of all humankind, not just the world of *man*.

C. Gregory Knight
The Pennsylvania State University
Editor, Resource Publications in Geography

Resource Publications Advisory Board

George W. Carey, *Rutgers University*
James S. Gardner, *University of Waterloo*
Charles M. Good, Jr., *Virginia Polytechnic Institute and State University*
Risa I. Palm, *University of Colorado*
Thomas J. Wilbanks, *Oak Ridge National Laboratory*

Preface

The literature on women and on women-men relationships is rich and varied. Hundreds of books, if not thousands, already exist on the subject, and the list grows rapidly. This recent popularity reflects society's awakening to the conditions of women throughout the world. Even a superficial perusal of the record reveals that women everywhere are disadvantaged relative to men. Not surprisingly, then, these sources usually point to discrimination and repression, and authors advocate changes to improve women's position.

This book is no exception. It is openly feminist. Many of the principle themes of feminist literature are examined below — economic discrimination, the double standard of permitted behavior, the invasion of female rights through the crime of rape, the unequal division of household labor. These and many other topics are discussed, some explicitly, some tangentially. Readers already familiar with the literature on feminism will therefore encounter many often-visited places. What feminists will find enlightening, we hope, is the reinterpretation of standard themes from a geographical perspective.

All the branches of knowledge dealing with people, in humanities and social sciences alike, have major publications on the subject of women. There are books on the psychology of women, the sociology of women, women and economics, women in history, and so forth. To date, however, no major publication has appeared on the subject of women written by a geographer. Many journal articles and professional papers exist (Zelinsky *et al.* 1982; Lee and Loyd 1982), but to our knowledge this is the first published geography monograph on feminist issues.

In part this situation is a function of the nature of geography and women's studies. Whereas a book on, say, *The History of the American Woman* seems quite understandable and logical from its title, a book on *The Geography of the American Woman* leaves the average reader confused. What could such a book involve? Geographies of other groups are less ambiguous — for example, *The Geography of the American Negro.* But until recently women seemed beyond the reach of a comprehensive geographical methodology. The result has been that many geographers continue to overlook half the world's population.

The purpose of this book (like all in this series) is to summarize recent scholarship on a subject for examination by the geographical community. In recent years the boundaries of geography have expanded to include much fascinating material which formerly was ignored. Issues of racism, poverty, and exploitation were discovered by geographers in the 1960s. Humanism, art, literature, and music were found to be geographically relevant in the 1970s. These and many other new topics which were incorporated into geography texts are important and valuable. Certainly, it is now time that geographers discover women. A review of geographical scholarship on women with a view toward future directions is highly appropriate.

It is also time that women (and those involved in women's studies) discover geography. While many specific issues examined below may be familiar to scholars well-read in feminism, the organizing structure is traditionally geographical and will be new to non-geographers. Geography, a science which seeks to explain phenomena located on the earth surface, organizes information in a spatial framework. Most non-geographers examine spatial relationships superficially, if at all, and the inter-relatedness of *place* is overlooked. Geographers endeavor to show the importance of attending to details of location, place, and spatial association.

In this book we concern ourselves with phenomena of human creation, thus de-emphasizing climate, landforms, and other elements of physical geography. Some of the fundamental questions asked by geographers are questions examined here with respect to women. Where are human beings located? Why are they there? How and why do they move from place to place? What do they think about with respect to their environment? How does the landscape reflect the presence of humans? This book, then, examines major themes of human geography by drawing from the literature of feminism. Our thanks are extended to Starr Sydell for her analysis of student mental maps and to Vince Carnazza for sharing accounts of explorations into traditionally female places.

Mary Ellen Mazey
David R. Lee

Contents

List of Figures

1

Where is She?

Perhaps the most obvious geographical issue in the study of women is a concern for patterns involving women or influenced by them. This problem has generated little research for the obvious reason that, with few exceptions, women are found where men are found, so the spatial patterns of women simply duplicate the general patterns of humankind. Communities of a single sex, female or male, are rare and small in size. Obviously, such communities can only survive one generation without importation of new members from outside. Single-sex communities do exist — monasteries and convents, women's and men's prisons come to mind — but these are small and exceptional. More generally, women locate with men.

The very fact that women live with men has profound social and political implications. Activists in the fight for sexual equality point out that inequality based on sex has numerous differences from racial inequality or discrimination based on religion. Ghettos, for all their faults, concentrate angry people in one place. Black ghettos have erupted from time to time as the anger of one citizen reinforces the anger of another. Sometimes anger brings change. When women are affronted they commonly become placated by kind words of men: fathers, husbands, lovers. These men are operating as cultural norms have taught them. For whatever reason, men do not fully comprehend the female's oppressed position. Consequently, the overall effect is that men and isolation defuse thousands of potentially explosive expressions of rage. It is when women begin meeting together to discuss their common histories of discrimination, to participate in consciousness raising exercises, that their anger can be expressed, channeled, and sometimes directed toward finding solutions.

Alice Rossie (1969:3-6) saw political implications inherent in the residential pattern of women as opposed to other groups:

> The Irish, the Italians, and the Jews in an earlier period, and blacks in more recent history, have been able to exert political pressure for representation and legislative change because residential concentration gave them voter strength in large urban centers. By contrast, women are for the most part evenly distributed throughout the population.

Since women live with men, there is potential conflict within families when women agitate for equality. To avoid conflict, they aquiesce or forbear. In part this explains why women, numerically a majority, continue to be treated as a minority.

Geography of the Sex Ratio

Studies of the location patterns of women cannot be concerned solely with places exclusively female. However, it is of interest to determine where women are in relatively greater numbers than men. This analysis becomes the geography of the sex ratio.

The sex ratio of a place as defined by the United Nations *Demographic Yearbook* is the number of males per 100 females (sex ratio = 100 • [males/females]). Figures greater than 100 show a high sex ratio, that is, more males than females; sex ratios below 100 indicate females are statistically dominant. Sex ratio at birth is high, approximately 105 males per 100 females. The female rate of survival is greater, and the sex ratio becomes balanced at about age four. Among the elderly the ratio is low because women live longer than men. The world average, considering all age groups, is nearly balanced (Gellis 1981; UNESCO 1978).

An unbalanced sex ratio may reflect many factors. Locales with high median age have a low (female-dominant) ratio. On the other hand, places which have a large proportion of the population younger than five years usually have high sex ratios. Imbalance also results from war, which selectively kills more men than women. Migration is another factor which creates imbalance in a place's sex ratio. In the 19th century, the American West in general had a very high sex ratio. Frontier areas offered opportunities to males in mines and ranches, but for women it was considered improper to strike out on one's own. An extreme case of an unbalanced sex ratio can be seen in California during the gold rush of the 1850s. Men outnumbered women more than 12 to 1 (sex ratio = 1228).

Rural-urban distinctions are usually significant. However, in some societies towns are heavily male, whereas in others the reverse is the case. For example, the towns of the United States have attracted females to work in generally low-paying factory and clerical jobs. Thus, the sex ratio of American urban communities is below the nation's average. In other societies, however men migrate to towns in great numbers for available jobs, leaving women to work the land. This is the case, for example, in parts of tropical Africa (Clark 1970:361). In the United States, the overall sex ratio was 93.2 in 1978; the ratio of the central cities was 88.8 whereas that of the rural farm population was 106.4 (U.S. Census 1980b: Table 1-4).

The world map of sex ratios shows the effect of many of these factors (Figure 1). Today, as in the past, harsh environments (the Arctic, deserts, high mountain zones) have very high sex ratios. In the Arctic fringe of North America, the sex ratio of Alaska, Yukon, and Northwest Territory has always been heavily dominated by males. This resulted from the sex selectivity of mining, forestry, and the military (Haglund 1969:278-87). Likewise Greenland's sex ratio is high (110); so too are the Falkland Islands near the southern tip of South America (123). The Norwegian possession of Svalbard, located well within the Arctic Circle, has a sex ratio of 287. High sex ratios are also found in the developing world: Pakistan (113), Angola (109), India and China (107) (UNESCO 1978). These high birth-rate countries have large numbers of very young children, which causes an imbalance toward male dominance.

In areas hardest hit by World War II, the sex ratio is markedly low. The Ukraine in the western part of the Soviet Union, for example, has the lowest sex ratio of any major world region (82.5). Other countries with a sex ratio of 90 or lower include Germany (both East and West), Austria, Byelorussia, and the U.S.S.R. proper. Smith (1977:188) argued that the low birthrate in the U.S.S.R. is due to Russian women fearing childbirth:

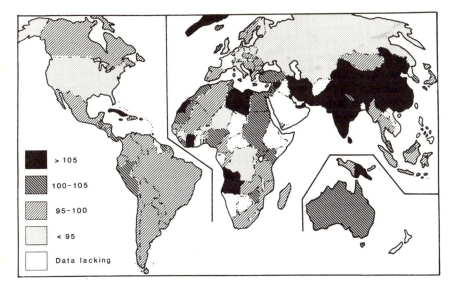

FIGURE 1   WORLD SEX RATIO, 1978 (UNESCO 1979).

"This is partly because little pain-killing anesthesia is used, but probably more fundamentally because of the archaic Soviet attitudes toward sex education and general preparation for birth." The United States has a moderately low sex ratio, though not so much the result of war as the effect of an aging population (UNESCO 1978).

Analysis of the sex ratio within national boundaries reveals many of the same influences which are important internationally. In the United States, mountain and desert areas, such as Nevada and Idaho, have higher-than-average sex ratios (Figure 2). Florida, with its large number of retirees, is low. Other southern states, such as Mississippi and Alabama, also have low sex ratios. This shows the effect of race: in general the U.S. black population has a lower sex ratio than the non-black population.

In a study of the 1970 U.S. population of 510 State Economic Areas, Gellis (1981) constructed a statistical model to explain variations in the sex ratio. He found that certain socio-economic variables explain a significant proportion of the variation in total sex ratio. Urban percentage was correlated negatively; that is, the more urbanized a district was, the lower was its sex ratio. Net migration was positively correlated, which corresponds to the theory that men migrate more than women. As migration rate goes up, so too does the sex ratio of a place. The racial variable (percentage black) was negatively correlated — as the percentage of the population of a district which is black increased, the sex ratio of that place decreased.

At the local level, other factors may become relevant. A male prison, for example, may be an important facility which raises the sex ratio of a county. The same effects result from the presence of a military base. In general, central cities have large numbers of females, whereas the sex ratio of the suburbs is more nearly balanced. The concentration of women in the cities reveals the presence of large numbers of female heads of households who cannot afford the price of a suburban house (Saegert 1980).

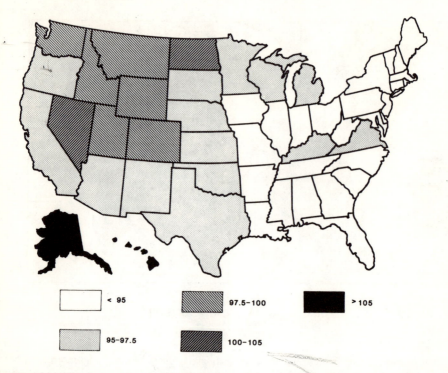

FIGURE 2   UNITED STATES SEX RATIO, 1980 (U.S. Census 1981, Table 3-5).

Low-cost housing is concentrated in the cities, and the job market is better. Since women depend more heavily than men on public transportation, women tend to locate where public transportation is available. A typical transit rider has been described as a middle-aged, low-income, black female. Moreover, day care centers and public services are more available in the cities than in the suburbs and rural areas. Among all major cities, Washington, DC has the lowest sex ratio (86.2 in 1980). This is due to a large segment of female employment in clerical sectors of the labor force as would be typical of many urban areas. Within the District, the female dominant areas had a large number of elderly persons and provided a large number of rental housing units (Birdsall and Gunville 1976).

Female Rights and Status

Female rights and status also exhibit spatial patterns. Alice Andrews devised a status-of-women index for countries for which data were available, combining the effects of fertility, life expectancy, and literacy. Status of women is highest in Western countries and slightly lower in Socialist countries. Status is lowest in parts of the Middle East, Asia, and tropical Africa (Andrews 1982). A similar analysis identified two types of female achievement, one which was a measure of social/educational status, the other of economic status (Figure 3). In general the patterns were similar to those reported by

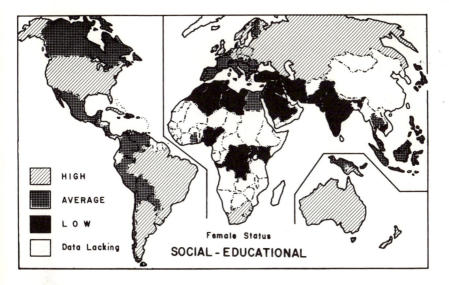

FIGURE 3 FEMALE STATUS. Top: social-educational status; bottom: economic status. (Reproduced from Lee *et al.* 1979 by permission of *Transition, Quarterly Journal of the Socially and Ecologically Responsible Geographers.*)

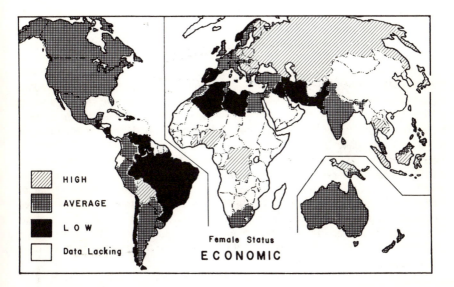

Andrews: high status for women in the West, poorer status in the Arab World and in India (Lee *et al.* 1979). The reasons for such spatial patterns are tied to economic and cultural factors.

Status levels of women in the United States have been suggested on the basis of income, educational, and occupational variables (Figure 4). Variables contributing to the index were median female earnings, percentage of adult female population with four or more years of college, and percentage of the female labor force classified as professional. Highest status occurs in the Northeast, the West, and the metropolitan areas. The rural South shows up as an area where women measure poorly in terms of these three variables (Lee and Schultz 1982). As with the world patterns, these national patterns are dependent on the economic and cultural characteristics of the various regions.

Since the emergence of the women's movement in the 1960s, women who wish to make a change in their living arrangements have found it difficult to do so because of the patriarchal orientation of local urban policy. Women have had to fight zoning ordinances that tend to prohibit the types of dwelling units which they prefer (Markusen 1981:34). An example of this can be found in a typical zoning ordinance that defines family as "one or more persons occupying a single dwelling unit, provided that unless all members are related by blood, adoption, or marriage, no such family shall contain over five persons" (Ohio Model Zoning Regulations 1973:10). By definition, then, two single women with two children each who live together are not a "family," so they would not be permitted by the zoning restrictions to form a household. Definitions of "family" and "household" such as this one can be found in the zoning ordinances of many suburban locations. More and more female single heads of households find it necessary to combine resources in order to maintain an acceptable standard of living, yet it is increasingly difficult to do so with such rigid and traditional zoning standards. It seems as though the struggles of women that center around housing, child care and even neighborhood preservation have been neglected in urban geography. These topics provide open arenas for future geographic research.

Women have a constant struggle in gaining equal access in the housing market. This is evident when discrimination is based on marital status, which is not barred by federal law. Under federal law a landlord may refuse to rent to all singles and divorced individuals, which include both males and females. Such restrictions are supposedly based on marital status, but in essence it is a form of sex discrimination since the prohibition is usually applied to women, not men (Taub and O'Kane 1981:185). Twenty-three states and the District of Columbia have enacted laws to prohibit sex discrimination in both real estate transactions and home finance, and sixteen of these and the District of Columbia also prohibit sex discrimination on the basis of marital status (Figure 5; Brown *et al.* 1977:279-85). The spatial distribution of these laws indicates that the liberal eastern and midwestern states along with the states in the West which have been in the forefront of women's rights continue to set the path for social change. Laws which prohibit sex discrimination in the housing area are conspicuously absent in the South.

Even in the area of employment some states have laws that place restrictions on women. Five states — Arkansas, Connecticut, Illinois, Louisiana, and Rhode Island — prohibit women from holding jobs in mines. Whether these are enforced is questionable. One restrictive law that is enforced in Michigan is known as a weight-lifting law. It prohibits giving a woman a task disproportionate to her strength. In only one state (New

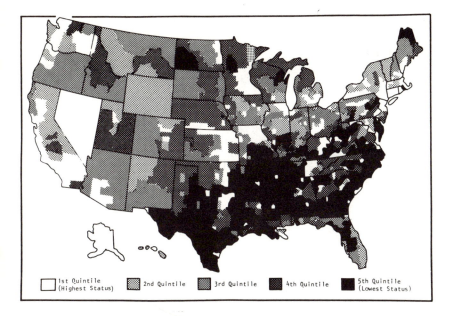

FIGURE 4   FEMALE STATUS IN THE UNITED STATES, 1970. Highest status indicates high absolute values of income, education and occupational variables. Data are shown by State Economic Areas (Lee and Schultz, 1982: Figure 1; reproduced by permission of *The Professional Geographer*).

Mexico) is there a sex-based maximum hours law that has not been declared invalid. This New Mexico law permits women to work overtime if the female signs an agreement to that effect (Brown *et al.* 1977:218).

For geographers, it is interesting to study the diffusion of these social changes in America toward women's rights and status. A number of spatial studies could be undertaken to examine changes in female's rights as they are intertwined with the cultural and social system of places. One attempt was made by Nancy Erwin (1978). She devised an overall index of women's legal equality based on an analysis of state laws which are discriminatory to women. The Mountain West and much of the South have a large number of laws which are generally considered unfair to women.

Spatial Patterns of the ERA

No issue has greater implications to women's equality than the Equal Rights Amendment to the U.S. Constitution. Originally introduced in 1923, the ERA finally passed the 92nd Congress in March of 1972. Thirty-eight states are required for ratification; thirty-five ratified leaving three needed when the amendment came to the end of its time deadline on June 30, 1982.

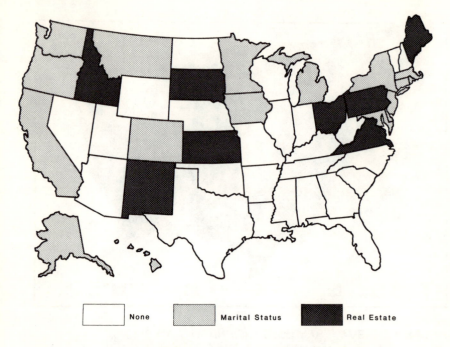

FIGURE 5   LAWS PROHIBITING SEX DISCRIMINATION IN HOUS-
ING. Twenty-four states and the District of Columbia have laws that
prohibit sex discrimination in both real estate transactions and home
finance (dark shading). Of these, seventeen states also prohibit discrimination on the basis of marital status (light shading). Unshaded states do
not have laws which prohibit sex discrimination both in real estate transactions and in home finance (data from Brown *et al.* 1977: Table 8.2)

The geography of ERA ratification shows interesting patterns (Figure 6). In 1972
twenty-one states ratified the amendment, Hawaii being the first. Many of these early
ratifiers were among the first states to have offered women suffrage, such as Colorado
which did so in 1896, Idaho (1896), California (1911), Kansas (1912), and New York
and Michigan (1917). In 1973 eight other states joined, bringing the total to twenty-nine.
These early-ratifying states, for the most part, are those usually considered liberal, the
Pacific states and the industrial Northeast. The late and non-ratifying states form two
definite concentrations: the Deep South and three states in the Mountain West
(Arizona, Utah, Nevada). Ironically, these three states were among the first to grant
women the right to vote — Utah (1896), Arizona (1912), and Nevada (1915). The
southern region of non-ratification reaches up the Mississippi and Ohio Valley to
Illinois, Indiana, and Ohio. In the West, Utah, Arizona, and Nevada form a contiguous
block of non-ratifying states, with Idaho and Nebraska expressing reservations by their
rescinding of the ratification. Obviously, these are states where the attitudes toward
women and women's place in society is that women are second to men. In Utah the
reason for non-ratification was religion, a Morman conviction that ERA would not be in

the best interests of women and the family. Yet neighboring Wyoming ratified the ERA in 1973. Wyoming stands at the forefront for women's rights in the United States since it was the first territorial legislature that granted women the right to vote. This was in 1869.

For the ERA to have become ratified, three of the fifteen non-ratifying states would have had to have voted in favor of the amendment. Feminists tried to influence the legislators in all the fifteen states. Political arguments were presented, to be sure, but economic pressures were tried as well, a tactic which goes back at least as far as the Boston Tea Party. One move was to discourage tourism and conventioning in unratified states, much to the consternation of such cities as New Orleans, Chicago, Miami, and Las Vegas. This "ERA boycott," as it is called, cost cities millions in tourist and convention revenue. The economic attacks on the cities of unratified states had little effect, however. Often state legislators from the cities already had voted to ratify, and it was the rural legislators who most staunchly opposed the constitutional amendment for equal rights.

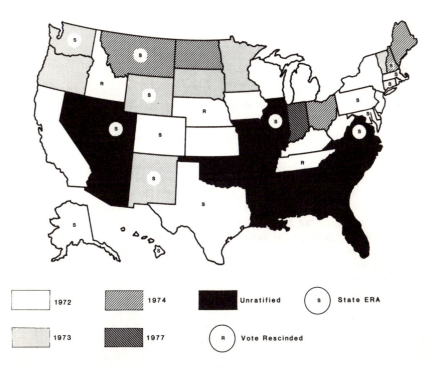

FIGURE 6   GEOGRAPHY OF THE EQUAL RIGHTS AMENDMENT. Shading indicates the year the Equal Rights Amendment to the U.S. Constitution passed in particular states. The dark pattern identifies states which did not ratify the ERA. R: states that ratified the amendment but later rescinded their vote. S: states that have adopted equal rights provisions to their state constitutions, though not all of them employ the same wording as the proposed federal amendment (data from *Time* 1977a and the National Organization of Women).

Where should feminists have concentrated their efforts? This question interested Wohlenberg (1979), who attempted to predict which non-ratifying states would be most likely to join the ranks of the ratified. His analysis was based on characteristics of the legislatures, the attitudes of the people, and the states' responses to earlier amendments (the Nineteenth and Twenty-sixth). The results suggested that a state's religious and political conservativism, and its response to earlier related amendments were the best predictors of which state would or would not ratify. The states with the greatest likelihood of passing the ERA were Arizona, Virginia, Illinois, Nevada, and Florida, in the that order. Those with the least likelihood were Mississippi, Alabama, South Carolina, Louisiana, and Utah. He demonstrated statistically what ERA activists had already recognized. Much effort and money went into those states which seemed to have the best chance, and in some of these states (Virginia, Illinois, Florida) success seemed almost at hand. Feminist organizations worked vigorously on the campaign, but so too did opponents, such as Phyllis Schlafly, who raised fears that the amendment would lead to the destruction of the family and to female military conscription. The deadline for ratification came, and the vote fell three states short. Immediately ERA activists began the campaign anew, keeping in mind their slogan: "ERA Won't Go Away."

The Geography of Disparity

The issue of female rights is closely intertwined with the matter of disparity. In this context, disparity is a comparison of the position occupied by the females of a population with that of the males, in terms of some attribute shared by both, such as education level, income, or mortality rate. Disparity then can be considered roughly equivalent to "inequality."

In India, there is great disparity in the levels of education between women and men. The literacy rates for both sexes vary greatly from region to region, but everywhere male literacy is higher. However, in those districts where overall literacy is high, the disparity between the sexes decreases. The north of India displays large disparity, and rural areas throughout the country have higher disparity of literacy than urban places. Certain cultural groups educate their women better than others: greater disparity is found among the highest caste Hindus (Brahmans) than among non-Brahman Hindus and Muslims (Sopher 1979).

Literacy in the United States is high for both sexes and the disparity of literacy rates is relatively insignificant. On other measures, however, such as median years of schooling or percentage of the population with a college degree, the education disparity between women and men is revealing. Where education levels are highest, the disparity between the sexes also is high. That is, the better educated people are, the greater the gap is between women and men (US Census, State Economic Areas, 1972). This contrasts with the Indian pattern noted above.

Disparity in women's status in the U.S. has also been measured (Figure 7). Variables used are those used in Figure 4 — income, education, and occupational status. In 1970, disparity was least in the rural South, largely because there is less status difference between black females and black males than between white females and white males. Disparity was high in the urbanized industrial belt of the northern states. Parts of the West also revealed high disparity. The Mountain states generally and the Mormon region specifically show great disparity between the status of men and

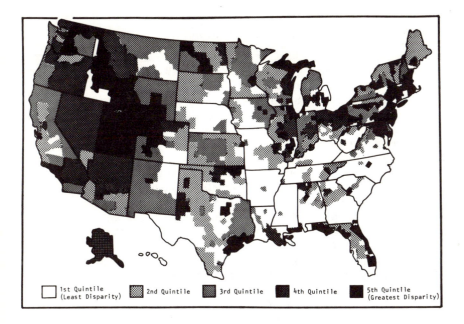

FIGURE 7   DISPARITY OF STATUS IN THE UNITED STATES, 1970.
Highest status indicates greatest male-female similarity; lowest status
indicates greatest disparity (Lee and Schultz 1982: Figure 3; reproduced
by permission of *The Professional Geographer).*

women. When the levels of disparity were compared with absolute scores for female
status (Figure 4), the correlation was significant. Where women were generally well off
in terms of education, income and occupation, the disparity between the sexes
nevertheless tended to be great. The correlation was even stronger between the
overall status of males and the disparity between females and males. This point bears
emphasizing: where men are well off — where they enjoyed high status — the
differences between the sexes (disparity of status) are *greatest*. Women do poorly
relative to the men where men are doing well. In those locales where men are well
educated, earning large salaries, and working in prestigious occupations, the gap
between these achievements for men and the achievements of women by the same
measure tends to widen. These results are startling and sobering. In places where
women have achieved economic and other successes, they are likely to find that their
male counterparts will have outdistanced them in terms of their own achievements. In
areas noted for political liberalism such as the suburban Northeast, where one might
reasonably have expected to find evidence of positive attitudes toward women, the
evidence seems to suggest the opposite (Lee and Schultz 1982:40).

Spatial Patterns of Abortion and Contraception

An individual's rights include the right to choose the destiny of one's body, specifically for women the right to choose to give birth or not. Abortion and contraception are emotionally charged matters regardless of what beliefs one might hold. Unquestionably, they are matters of great importance.

Until recently, most countries denied legal sanction to abortion. Notwithstanding, the practice of abortion is and has been pervasive, irrespective of legality. A survey of world societies revealed that abortion is absolutely ubiquitous throughout the world. We cannot even mentally construct a society where women would not abort, or at least feel compelled to abort (Devereux 1967:98). Abortion is a universal characteristic of human populations and not some aberration resulting from recent societal changes.

Women around the world terminate pregnancies, some legally and safely, too many by relying on dangerous, illegal means. The spatial patterns of abortion practices can be examined by two criteria, the legal status of abortion and the actual extent, or rate of abortion. The rate of abortion (number of abortions per 1000 births in a year) is high in Socialist countries, almost without exception (Figure 8). In part, this is a function of female employment and reflects the greater opportunity (and usual necessity) for women to seek employment outside the home than is the case in the West. High female employment in Eastern Europe is related to the very low sex ratio resulting from death of males in World War II and the fear of childbirth mentioned above. The weak influence of religious sanctions is likewise a factor of importance, as is the general prevalence of

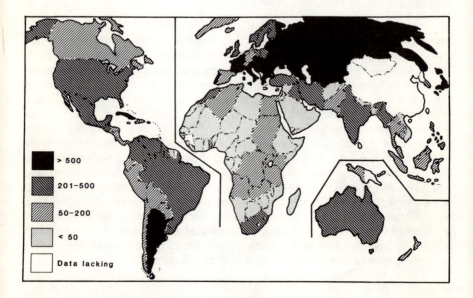

FIGURE 8   WORLD ABORTION RATE, 1976. Abortions (legal and illegal) per 1,000 live births (after map in *People* 1978).

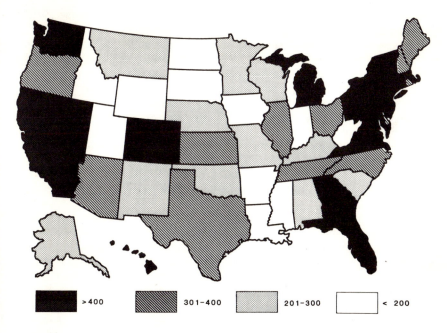

FIGURE 9   U.S. ABORTION RATE, 1978. Legal abortions per 1,000 live births (U.S. Census 1980a).

high quality, low-cost medical care. Contraception and abortion are widely practiced in Socialist countries. In the Soviet Union, the main method of birth control is abortion. Birth control devices are legal but in short supply and of poor quality. For each birth there are two abortions, according to one source (Smith 1977:189). The impact of the high abortion rate in the U.S.S.R. is that the birth rate of the European population in the U.S.S.R. (mainly Russians) is quite low — some Soviet national planners view this demographic fact with great alarm.

High use of contraception practices and moderately high abortion rates characterize Western nations; the United States fits this pattern (Figure 9). Abortions became legalized in this country in 1973. The rate of abortion per 1000 live births in the following year was 282 nationwide. By 1977 it increased 42 percent to 400 per 1000 births. The rate is highest in the Middle Atlantic States (New York, New Jersey, Pennsylvania) and in the states of the Pacific Coast. In Washington, DC there are more abortions than births. Abortion is lowest in the South and in the Rocky Mountain states. In a very general sense the patterns of abortion rates corresponds with a liberal-conservative bias in the population. Rates are highest in liberal areas (the Northeast, the Pacific states, the District of Columbia) and low in conservative areas (the South, the Upper Middle West, Utah). However, the correlation does not seem to be strong, indicating that the propensity toward termination of pregnancy cannot be explained so simply.

In Western Europe the abortion rate is also high. Italy is an interesting case. Before restrictive laws were relaxed in 1978, abortion (strongly opposed by the Roman Catholic Church) was illegal. Moreover, contraceptive methods were not widely used.

Yet the abortion rate was high, estimated at 200 to 750 per 1000 live births. Though the termination of a pregnancy was legally punishable, it is estimated that only one in 50,000 abortions would come before the courts. At present, the laws are similar to those in the United States (*People* 1978; Population Crisis Committee 1979).

In Latin America, abortion is comparable to that of Italy prior to legal reform: high rate of abortion while contraception practice is low. As will be discussed below, nowhere is abortion on demand permitted, and some countries in Latin America have very restrictive abortion laws. The consequences of large numbers of illegal abortions are staggering though predictable. The death rate for women who have undergone illegal abortions is estimated to be from 100 to 1000 deaths per 100,000 cases. This rate is higher than the death rate resulting from complications in the delivery of live births (250-800 per 100,000). The death rate associated with legal abortions is relatively miniscule: 4-6 deaths per 100,000. In Latin America and throughout the world where laws are restrictive, women die tragically in large numbers when they attempt to terminate a pregnancy using unsafe devices and practices. In Colombia, the largest maternity hospital in Bogota must devote half its beds to cases arising from complications of illegally induced abortions (*Science News* 1976). The situation is also bad in Mexico City: four beds in five in the Women's Hospital are filled by women suffering from abortion complications.

Low abortion rates, often found with low use of contraceptives, are found in the poor nations of the world, especially in Africa and the Middle East. Many Middle Eastern areas lack the medical facilities to perform safe abortions, but religion is probably the more decisive reason for the pattern. Most of the countries having the lowest abortion rates have Muslim majorities or significant Muslim minorities. Islam, like Catholicism, condemns the practice of abortion.

The map of abortion laws (Figure 10) reveals some unexpected patterns. Latin America, in spite of the influences of Catholicism, shows varied patterns. Some countries in Central and South America (such as Colombia) have adopted very restrictive laws, but others allow abortion with certain restrictions. Subsaharan Africa displays mixed attitudes, which seem to be drawn on old colonial lines. Zaire, for example, has extremely restrictive laws, as does Belgium, its former colonial master. Former English colonies (Zimbabwe, Zambia, Kenya, Uganda, Ghana) are less restrictive than former French ones, such as Senegal, Ivory Coast, and Upper Volta.

Though data are lacking for much of the Muslim world, this region overall is quite restrictive. Tunisia is a liberal exception, but among Islamic nations Tunisia is one of the most westernized. In general, restrictive status is the rule in the Muslim World from Algeria on the west to Indonesia on the east.

The legal status of abortion is most liberal in the Socialist countries. In the Republic of China and in the countries of the Soviet bloc, abortion is available on request or with only minimum restrictions. Western Europe overall exhibits a liberal attitude as well, as does the English-speaking world, including the United States.

Though the United States has liberalized abortion laws, the number of people who oppose abortion is substantial. Therefore abortion continues to be a volatile issue in this country, even at the local level. Abortion clinics are picketed by opponents; ironically, some have even been bombed by violent right-to-life protesters. In 1982 the director of an abortion clinic and his wife were kidnapped by an obscure group calling itself "The Army of God." After one week the couple were released, but the incident took grave psychological tolls on the nation's abortion clinics (Wohl 1982:19). The U.S.

Supreme Court has guaranteed that no state or locality may prohibit the right for a woman to terminate a pregnancy, but restrictions may be placed on where clinics and hospitals may be sited. Abortion clinics, just as all facilities performing a community service, must meet local zoning laws. So when a new clinic is proposed in a community, not uncommonly the question of where such a clinic may be located becomes the source of heated debate.

The example of Deerfield Beach, Florida, may be typical of many communities. Deerfield Beach is a middle class community along the Atlantic Ocean in southeastern Florida. In 1981, the Deerfield Beach Medical Center attempted to obtain a license to open a proposed clinic which would perform a wide range of gynecological services, including abortions. City commissioners were faced with some 150 abortion opponents. The issue supposedly being discussed was whether the zoning regulations permitted a clinic to function in the specific site in question. However, the arguments over licensing centered less on the fine points of local land use restrictions than on the morality issue of who has more rights, an adult woman or a fetus.

Closely associated with the matter of abortion is that of contraception. In the United States, attitudes toward contraception are fairly liberal. This is less the case in France, however. In a study of the Strasbourg region, Rimbert and Vogt (1978) interviewed women in order to construct a map of attitudes toward contraception. Definite regional

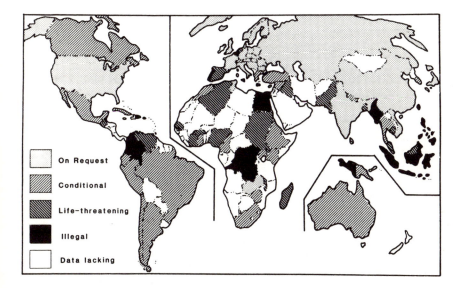

FIGURE 10 LEGAL STATUS OF ABORTION, 1978. On request: abortions granted on request or under a broad range of social conditions. Conditional: abortion permitted only under certain conditions, including eugenic, rape, incest, and/or broad health indications. Life-threatening: abortions are granted only if woman's life is threatened. Illegal: abortions are illegal, with no exceptions (from data in Population Crisis Committee 1979).

differences were identified. Opponents generally were from rural areas or small towns. The typical opponent spoke a regional dialect (as opposed to metropolitan French), had four or more children, and was poorly informed about contraception in general. Women who expressed greatest favor with contraception were from the large regional city of Strasbourg or its suburbs, or were from other smaller urban places. Such women typically spoke standard French, they read regional or national newspapers, and their husbands were managers or professionals. Attitudes were strongly divided along social class lines: women of the higher classes were in favor of birth control. The maps of contraception attitudes mirrored more general maps of overall cultural characteristics of the Strasbourg region. This regional correspondence is predictable since feelings about contraception are influenced by deeper cultural patterns.

Other Spatial Patterns

A variety of locational issues relating to women have been analyzed. Other spatial patterns await further study, some of which we can suggest here.

Regional patterns in fertility were examined in Sri Lanka. Investigators discovered that fertility rates were not satisfactorily explained by socio-economic variables, but visual map comparisons revealed a close association between fertility and climate. However, "a climatological explanation of fertility is less than intellectually satisfying and, more to the point, not particularly useful." (Fuller et al. 1980). The climate issue did, however, suggest ecologically related causes, and the researchers found a significant linkage between incidence of malaria and fertility. Similar studies may be useful in other developing areas.

The female work force varies from country to country and from region to region, providing yet another challenge to geographical analysis. Women are a large part of the labor force in the West, in Japan, and in the Socialist bloc. The percentage of women who are employed is lowest in strongly Catholic countries and in the World of Islam. In these latter regions there is strong pressure to support the notion that "a woman's place is in the home." Husbands feel a working wife reflects badly on their image as providers. In the United States, approximately half the women of working age are employed. In urban areas women constitute a larger percentage of the work force than in non-urban areas. In part, this reflects the greater variety of opportunities women have for employment in urban factories and offices than in rural establishments. Race is also significant. In predominantly black locales, women are a larger part of the work force than in non-black areas. Local variations can be found to these general statements. In Tennessee, the labor force engaged in manufacturing is more than 50 percent female in large parts of the state, especially in rural areas. In and around urban areas, women are a third or less of the manufacturing labor force. The high percentage of women in rural manufacturing is related to the low wage structure of rural centers. Married women are willing to seek employment, even at low wages, because their husbands' salaries are low and the additional money is needed to support the household (Klimasewski 1974).

Although the percentage of women enumerated as participating in the labor force is lower in developing countries, particularly in Latin America, the statistics do not always portray a realistic description. In these countries, and even developed countries, women are commonly relegated to positions in the "informal" labor force, working as neither government nor wage-earning employees. Occupations such as street vendors, prostitutes and domestic servants, usually the work of women, are considered non-market activities, and therefore are not counted as a part of a country's GNP.

In addition to the urban examples of informal labor force activity, it has been found, particularly in Africa, that women are a major contributor to agricultural activity (Boserup 1970). This, too, was the case in early frontier settlement of the United States (Faragher 1979:50-59). In many African societies, all tasks connected with food production continue to be left to women. It is rather ironic that as European colonization took place in Africa and agricultural mechanization was introduced, agricultural work became more masculine as it became less physical, while women became associated with roles that were domestically oriented. Cross-culturally, a higher percentage of females participate in the agricultural systems of Africa and some Southeast Asia countries such as Thailand and Cambodia than in Latin America and the Arab World. One reason may be the greater importance of wage labor in Latin America and the Arab World as compared to Africa and Southeast Asia (Boserup 1970).

The western, industrialized world has a high percentage of women involved in the labor force, but the occupational segregation is such that numbers and totals are misleading. Whether women are employed as white-collar workers or blue-collar workers, they are clustered in relatively few occupations. This factor alone has spatial implications. Since women are occupationally clustered it can be assumed that this limits their access to the location and place of work.

Other factors influence the female's labor force participation. The role of fertility has been examined. Although it is well documented that an increasing number of mothers with young children are working, it is still true that the younger the child at home, the less likely it is the mother will work (Kadushin 1980; Hayghe 1973).

Fertility and female participation in the labor force involve not only the working mother and the age of the children, but also the number of children. As the number of women in the labor force has increased, the birth rate has fallen. Therefore, it has been concluded that there is a negative relationship between maternal employment and the family size (Waldman and Gover 1971; Hoffman 1974). An interesting study could be done to develop the spatial implications of these findings. Additionally, it has been found that the level of education is indirectly and/or directly related to women's labor force participation (Hoffman 1974). Again, a number of geographical studies could be formulated to compare such spatial relationships and variations at a micro or macro scale.

2

Where Does She Go?

An interest in spatial patterns and map distributions does not constrain the geographer to view the landscape as static and unchanging. Equally important to the science of geography are patterns of movement and change over space. Questions of transportation and migration present themselves, as do problems of the spread of innovations from one locale to another. In this chapter these issues are examined as they apply to women.

Diffusion

Diffusion is the spread of an innovation from one place to another. In the 18th and 19th centuries most innovations in America originated in the technologically advanced East and diffused to the frontier. Female suffrage, however, originated in the West, in Wyoming in 1869 (Figure 11). Utah quickly (and, from today's perspective, uncharacteristically) followed suit. The diffusion wave spread to neighboring regions as other western states agreed that women should have the constitutional right to vote. Then the innovation leaped to a noncontiguous state, Illinois (1913), and spread outward from both the western hearth and from the new Middlewest node. Finally, all but the southern states had ratified the constitutional amendment of 1920 (Figure 11). This diffusion pattern was tied to the cultural attitudes toward women at this particular time in American history.

Easing restrictions on divorce likewise originated in Wyoming and spread in a manner similar to suffrage throughout the West, although a barrier effect was encountered in Roman Catholic New Mexico. Illinois again represented a secondary node as the innovation leaped ahead of the diffusion wave. Gould noted the similarities of the two diffusion patterns and speculated that other reform issues would follow a similar pattern. From his 1969 perspective, abortion reform seemed to be on the verge of such a diffusion pattern:

> We might speculate that many reform movements follow similar paths of diffusion, and that they will continue to do so in the future. Abortion reform, for example, has been passed in Colorado and is on the legislative dockets in many other western states; this reform movement may also spread along channels that seem to be very stable over time (Gould 1969:64).

As it worked out, it was New York, an eastern state, which first passed relaxed anti-abortion statutes. Norah Henry studied the diffusion of abortion facilities in the northeast to attempt to determine the pattern of diffusion from the New York hearth. Local abortion laws were influential in explaining when abortion facilities reached a community, but income levels and local opposition to abortion had no significant effect. The diffusion pattern was as follows: initially it spread as a wave outward from New York City, then leaped to the Chicago area, and finally spread from both major urban centers down the urban size hierarchy from larger to ever smaller urban places (Henry 1979). As a contemporary issue for women, abortion seems to have originated in urban areas that are linked to liberal viewpoints and, therefore, are on the forefront of women's rights.

Information on abortion is relatively easy to obtain in this country, but this is not the case where abortion is illegal or strongly restricted. In Chile, for example, abortions are performed in illegal clinics: how, then, would a pregnant woman learn of the location of clandestine facilities (of which there are many)? This question concerned Gary Fuller, who gathered data in Santiago. By inspecting records of these illegal abortion clinics he found that innovation waves were generated in a regular and periodic fashion. Information that a new clinic was available spread out in the manner of waves from the site of the clinic to the streets of Santiago. The waves affected only small areas and were directionally biased, more or less restricted in the direction of their flow. Fuller attempted to see which of the many theoretical diffusion models might best describe the actual Santiago case. Most of the usual models were unsatisfactory to explain the

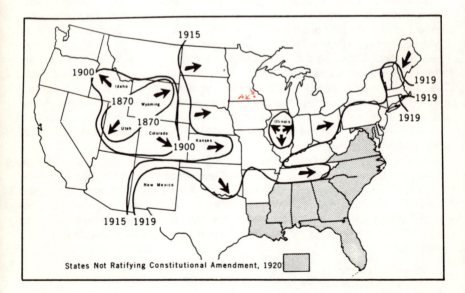

FIGURE 11   DIFFUSION OF PRESIDENTIAL SUFFRAGE FOR WOMEN, 1870-1920. Illinois granted suffrage in 1913 (Gould 1969: Figure 68, p. 63).

diffusion pattern of information about clandestine clinics, but a climatology diffusion model worked well. This model, developed originally to explain the distribution of pollutants spreading out downwind from a smokestack, also worked in describing the spread of the diffusion waves outward from clinics into the streets of Santiago (Fuller 1973). The implication of this finding is that information on illicit activities (abortion information in this case) diffuses according to patterns we do not yet fully understand. The mechanisms appear unlike those of other cultural diffusions and, at present, can only be described using analogies from the physical world.

In Guatemala, where safe, legal abortions are not available to peasant women, traditional methods are used to induce abortion. In their folklore, menstruation is "the effect of the moon." If a woman has lost the effect of the moon and does not want children (and in one survey 80 percent said they wanted no more children), she would contact her mother or another woman (never her husband directly) to learn of traditional abortion techniques. Communication on family planning matters and female physiology occurs freely between women but practically never between women and men. The two sexes live spatially in the same world but simultaneously are separated by a rigid set of social barriers to communication (Early 1980). Obviously, this relationship is tied to cultural traditions of physical space and psychological space in Guatemalan society.

These findings on illegal abortion information and facilities illustrate the existence of information exchange systems which flourish outside the established communication channels. Information exchange networks operate to diffuse information on sensitive or taboo subjects. Network analysis has been investigated from a theoretical standpoint; only recently has the concept been applied in a feminist context however. Farnsworth (1980:24) brought the importance of networks to the attention of geographers:

> In the '70s, many women's groups have formally discovered networking.
> They are beginning to use networking in a conscious attempt to access
> information and attain a greater control over events which effect them.

Networks are of concern to geographers, says Farnsworth, "because distance factors play a very important part in casual exchanges — and so many of these women's groups are making extraordinary efforts to overcome distance" (Farnsworth 1980:24).

Numerous types of networks are available for women. One is the network designed to provide information about employment and economic opportunities. This type of networking "seems likely to become the feminist phenomenon of the 1980s" (Wilson 1980). Such networks disseminate information about employment opportunities to women who might otherwise not learn of them. One of the major complaints of women seeking employment, especially of a professional or managerial nature, is that they never learn of jobs for which they may qualify, so they do not apply. Jobs are offered by male employers to other male applicants through an "old boy network," a network of men who are friends, or friends of friends, and may have gone to school together (they wear the "old school tie"). Such applicants may or may not be as qualified as the woman candidate, but importantly, they are socially acceptable. When jobs go to social contacts, women are excluded because usually the male employer's friends are themselves men. The affirmative action movement of the 1970s was designed by Federal legislation to break these male-only networks: employers would be compelled to make an affirmative effort to promulgate notices of jobs to all groups who traditionally had been excluded, including women.

Federal guidance with affirmative action may indeed lead, eventually, to equality in employment. In the meantime, non-governmental networks — national, state and local — have been designed to spread the word to women about matters which may affect them economically. The importance of networks of this type is realized in a very real and immediate sense by feminists in the geography profession. At present, three regional and two national newsletters are printed which are directed toward women in the profession. At regional and national conferences feminists meet to disseminate information to women and to identify women not yet a part of the network so that they may become aware of opportunities for advancement. Similar types of networks are to be found in other professional organizations.

Another function of networks is to provide some unity to groups whose members are spatially separated. America is a complex society consisting of thousands of groups with special interests, beliefs, and life-styles. In order to survive, special-interest communities develop strategies to maintain support systems and establish places where they can comfortably meet. Bonnie Loyd studied one such community, the San Francisco community of radical feminists. The community had a large potential membership but it was scattered throughout the San Francisco Bay area. This led to the development of the Women's Switchboard in 1972. The Switchboard provided information on housing, medical care, crafts and skills, and mental health issues. The telephone permitted the feminist community to expand in spite of the lack of propinquity of its members (Loyd 1977; Loyd and Rowntree 1978).

At the national level another type of feminist information/action network is the National Organization for Women (NOW). In 1970, this organization had 3,000 members in thirty cities. Ten years later it expanded to 741 chapters and some 120,000 members. The central office is in Washington, DC. Each state has a state-level office. Information and resources flow from one level of organization to the others. Items of concern at the national level may be disseminated from the national headquarters to state and local chapters, or to the members directly via a newsletter and other publications. Likewise information flows from a community or state to the national office. For example, local people inform the national office of critical feminist issues of concern to the community. Resources flow from individuals in the form of dues and special contributions to support the local chapter as well as the state national levels to support local feminist issues, such as the election of local feminist candidates.

Both in a theoretical and in a real-world sense, information can reach individual NOW members rapidly, thanks to the ubiquity of the telephone. The local NOW chapter president (acting on information coming from state or national NOW headquarters, or in response to some local stimuli) activates the "telephone tree." The president phones two or three members; they in turn phone two or three others, and rapidly the total chapter membership is informed of an important issue which may require quick action. For example, in the case of the clinic in Deerfield Beach, Florida, the City Council denied a license to a clinic to perform abortions. Within a day, the Broward County Chapter of NOW had activated its membership and pressure was brought to bear on the council to reverse its decision.

Networks of this kind have been important long before modern communication technology permitted near-instantaneous dissemination of information. Mary Ryan described the Female Moral Reform Society, which sought to reform standards of sexual behavior and eliminate sexual violence. It had more than 400 chapters in the Northeast in the 1830s and 1840s. Cities with chapters sometimes served satellite groups in nearby communities. Though the pace of life was slower, information still was disseminated through informal women's channels. Today's equivalent to such early feminist movements, Ryan speculates, is not so much the contemporary feminist organizations as the anti-feminist networks. These organizations she calls the New Right:

> *Through neighborhood organization and affiliation with local and national churches, these women of the 1970s are conducting yet another campaign to control sexual mores: attacking homosexuality, fighting abortion and the ERA, and venerating the heterosexual nuclear family (Ryan 1979:82).*

From the feminist point of view, the anti-feminist networks have a powerful advantage over feminist ones. In today's world, the female feminist quite often is a very busy woman, with job, family, and feminist causes competing for her attention. Anti-feminists extoll the virtues of the woman-at-home model of female behavior, which allows time for a variety of activities in addition to housework. Feminist organizations all too often find that highly qualified and committed women simply cannot spare the time for social action. This is seldom the case among anti-feminists who are not employed away from the home.

Daily Spatial Activity Patterns

Short range movements, movement patterns which take place on a day to day basis, reveal much about how a society organizes space. They also tell how differently the two sexes operate in space. Essentially, the pattern is this: men's trips are farther and last longer than those of women, especially when the women are non-employed housewives.

In terms of overall travel, men average 65 percent more travel time than women (Robinson 1977). Men drive more than women: nearly three-quarters of the U.S miles driven are by men (Guiliano 1979:609). Some 87 percent of men hold driver's licenses, compared to 62 percent of women. Those women who are licensed to drive, moreover, are less likely to have access to private automobiles, further restricting their mobility. In one study, 81 percent of the men (but only 47 percent of the women) had direct access to a car (reported in Palm and Pred 1978:23).

Even though women drive less, they are safer drivers than men. In a California study, women's driving performance was found to be three times better than that of men. The female superiority held for all age groups except the very elderly, among whom driving performance was about the same for both sexes. Insurance companies typically assess young female drivers (ages 16-25) at approximately one-half the premium of young male drivers. These facts demonstrate the fallacy of jokes about "women drivers," how they are supposedly unpredictable and therefore dangerous.

Generally women travel less than men, but women use busses and other forms of public transportation to a greater degree than men. Most Americans find public transportation less satisfactory than the private automobile. In general, then, women lack the freedom to go where and when they want compared with men.

Housewives travel the least, whereas employed men travel the most. Employed women fall midway between these two groups. Housework and child care by and large tie one to the home, so the restricted travel patterns of housewives are not surprising.

However, some housework chores require travel outside the home (grocery and other shopping trips, travel to the repair shop, etc.). It is revealing that when men do help with housework, they are far less likely to work in the home than to do the shopping and other travel-related chores. Housewives do spend more time than men in shopping and other travel-related housework, 64 percent more, but when it comes to the strictly homebound jobs, housewives spend a whopping 659 percent more time than men on these jobs!

In one respect men are disadvantaged. Both housewives and husbands spend time visiting friends, but women spend more time visiting than men, more than half again as much. Likewise, women make more social trips than men (Wheeler and Stutz 1971:399). However, such trips are short; women's friends tend to live close to home, men's farther away (Everitt 1976; Stutz, 1976:6-7). These data fulfill the stereotype that women have traditionally been tied to the domestic sphere of society while men are more tied to the public sphere. As more women become employed in the labor force, and more men take responsibility for household activities, these statistics will more than likely change.

In a normal development cycle of a person, the "activity space," the area around home which contains most of the places visited in a day's time, increases through childhood and reaches its greatest extent during the individual's productive years. The female's activity space is usually smaller than that of her male counterparts. Tognoli (1979:600-601) summarized research on this subject that indicated that boys at play range significantly farther from home than girls; at work, boys are apt to have jobs which take them into the out-of-doors (paper routes, lawn mowing), whereas girls will have indoor tasks (baby-sitting, for example). Anderson and Tindall (1972:1, 4-5) found similar results. Girls and boys in their early teens have somewhat comparable travel routines, but when they reach sixteen and are able to drive, boys far more than girls are given the opportunity to use a car and thus can range farther from home (Fava 1980:138-9). By college age, however, women find new freedom. Sex-linked differences in spatial behavior are probably least among young adults. A study of university students showed that females hitchhiked and walked after dark less often, but made shopping trips more often than men. On other measures no difference was noted, and overall the spatial mobility was about the same for both sexes (Loyd 1973).

Activity space expands for men after college as they take jobs and then rise in their professions. This may also be true for the employed woman, but not so for the housewife/mother. Her world shrinks as more and more she attends to domestic and neighborhood matters. Later in life activity space contracts both for women and men. However, this shrinkage is gradual for women and usually fairly inconsequential from about middle age on. With men, however, the shrinkage becomes dramatic with retirement. Men who formerly incorporated much travel in a day's time suddenly have their activity space reduced to a size similar to that of their wives — with the effect of depression among many retired men (Holcomb and Parkoff 1980).

Urbanization affects activity patterns. Risa Palm, who examined travel patterns in Colorado communities, found that women in small towns spend two or three times more time in travel than do women in urban or suburban America. Much of this is seen as a tedious burden, and Palm sympathized with their plight: "Although the chauffeuring of children to the orthodontist may seem burdensome to the suburban housewife, just imagine the burden this trip creates for the person who must drive three or more hours" (Palm 1979:130). The smaller the community, Palm found, the more time that women must spend traveling. This is because smaller communities can support fewer services and establishments. Therefore, depending on particular situations, women may have tremendous burdens placed upon them due to place of residence.

Working women in Palm's Colorado sample had about twice the leisure time of urban and suburban employed women, but this figure is misleading. Many local industries such as mining and construction are denied to women. Moreover, professional women find little opportunity for employment locally. Thus there is much underemployment and, therefore, surplus leisure time (Palm, 1979, Table 5). This leisure time may not occur by choice but rather because women have constrained opportunities.

When a woman takes on outside employment, she is seldom relieved of the household tasks. Rather, the outside job is added onto domestic chores. The husband rarely increases his share of the housework when the wife takes on a job outside the home. One comparison between data of the mid 1960s and 1973 showed that the number of husbands who provided no help whatsoever around the house actually increased 46 percent, and the number who did help out at least five hours per week decreased by 31 percent (Robinson 1977). Glazer-Malbin, who reviewed housework studies, noted "that husbands of employed wives do very little housework compared with their wives, and that the amount of housework done by such husbands is similar to the amount done by husbands of unemployed wives (Glazer-Malbin 1976). Moreover, among husbands who did help with housework, that help characteristically is in areas deemed most interesting and satisfying: cooking and shopping as compared, for example, with ironing, tidying, laundering, and similar tasks which rank low in terms of satisfaction (Oakley 1974). Shopping involves travel outside the home. As noted above, men do more shopping than stay-at-home housework. This again shows the male tradition of orientation toward the public sphere while females are tied to the tasks associated most strongly with the domestic sphere. Tognoli (1979:600) finds in these house work patterns far reaching implications of tremendous importance:

> In general, men's separation from the house and from domestic work creates in them a sense of alienation and contributes to a negative relationship between women and men and between men and their children . . . Not only is such rigidity [of roles] likely to push boys outside the home when they do not necessarily want to be there, but it also encourages needless adventure-seeking and bravado, which subsequently can enhance a destructive competitiveness in boys and men which is not as present among girls or women.

The competition for the energies of the employed housewife greatly limits the amount of time she can spend away from home; often this limits the time she can spend in commuting to work. Married working women travel shorter distances to work than unmarried working women (Ericksen 1977:430), and working women spend less time traveling to work (38 percent less) than employed men (Robinson 1977). In a Los Angeles study, Everitt graphically showed the differences in the size and shape of behavioral space maps between employed women and men (Figure 12). Men traveled 29 percent farther to work than women and their work places spread out in many directions from their home. Women's work places were closer and more directionally biased than the men's (Everitt 1976:108-9). In a Dayton, Ohio, study the average number of miles traveled to place of employment for women was 8.7 (14 kilometers); for men, 11.8 miles (19 kilometers; Mazey and Seiler n.d.). Likewise, in a Canadian study the figures were 9 miles (14.5 kilometers) for women, 13 miles (20.9 kilometers) for men (Cichocki 1980:156). These data indicate that women's choice of employment may be spatially constricted and influenced by proximity to home. These geographical relationships need to have more empirical investigation.

The comparative lack of mobility of the married woman may mean that she is unable to accept a position at a rank and salary commensurate with her abilities if the employment site lies distant from her home. This problem was examined by J. F. Madden. When wife and husband are employed, both would prefer jobs near home. But the wife, because of the many demands on her time, is more willing than the husband to accept lower wages for employment in a firm near her home. This situation "yields a female labor supply curve that is less elastic than the male supply. In this case it is

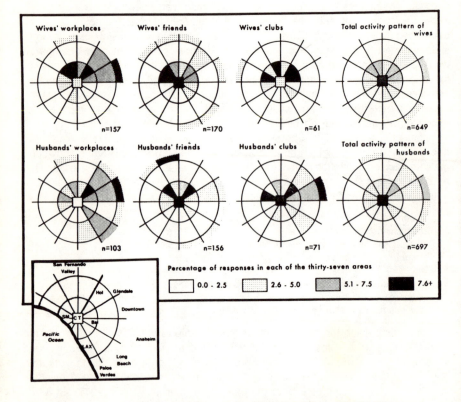

FIGURE 12   DISTRIBUTION OF WORKPLACES, FRIENDS' HOMES, CLUBS, AND TOTAL ACTIVITY PATTERNS OF WIVES AND HUSBANDS AMONG A WEST LOS ANGELES STUDY GROUP. Inset, location of study census tract (CT) and surrounding communities: Santa Monica (SM), Baldwin Hills (Bal), Los Angeles International Airport (LAX) and Hollywood (Hol). (Reproduced from Everitt 1976: Figures 2 and 3, by permission of *Annals, Association of American Geographers*).

obviously optimal for the employer to pay women less than men . . ." (Madden 1977:380). Data such as these show that women's increase in labor force participation has not brought equal access to the labor market.

Women in suburban England illustrate Madden's point. When women with small children decided to return to work, there is a decline in occupational status, as former secretaries take on typing duties and women from all fields take on duties as cleaners and baby-sitters (Tivers 1977:18). As with the small-town women of Colorado, under-employment is high: the majority of women in the England study were employed less than thirty hours per week. This validates previous findings that indicate the occupational segregation of women and the fact that they comprise the majority of the part-time labor force. During the world wars, women were considered to be the "reserve" labor force; it seems today that they have only moved a small step ahead of that secondary position.

The effect of lack of mobility on choice of work place was also demonstrated by J. Meyer in her study of Montessori teachers, 98 percent of whom are women. The teachers entered their profession from one of four walks of life: educators in other systems, employed women in non-education professions, students, and homemakers. When asked why they chose their first position, 81 percent of the homemakers replied because the position was near their home. The appealing philosophical foundation of the Montessori education system, or attractive considerations of the working environment were given by only 16 percent. On the other hand, among the non-homemakers, propinquity to home was only given by 34 percent of the respondents, whereas philosophical and environmental considerations were the reasons among 36 percent. Among students, philosophical/environmental reasons were the highest: 56 percent of them chose their first Montessori position on these idealistic bases. When women become homemakers, domestic propinquity displaces idealism when it comes to choice of location for work place (Meyer 19;75:55-9).

One major constraint to mothers who wish to enter the labor force is the availability of child-care services. In the suburban England study, for example, poor child-care facilities kept many women from working who otherwise would choose to do so. Those women who least required the use of day care facilities were able to commute to London for better jobs, whereas those with great day care needs took mediocre jobs in the local area (Tivers 1977:15-16). Pred and Palm illustrate the problem graphically using daily time-space "prisms," two-dimensional geometric constructions which illustrate the distance an individual can conveniently travel from home in a normal working day. The farther that individual must travel to jobs, or the more stops they must make en route, the less time they can allot to employment. Pred and Palm's hypothetical individual "Jane" had a time-space prism which must accommodate both a workday and a drive to a day care center. Her choice of jobs was greatly restricted by the constraint imposed by the travel to the day care center (Figure 13; Pred and Palm 1978). These data, too, illuminate the spatial implications and constraints placed upon women as they increase their labor force participation.

J. Monk also presented the problem from the standpoint of the time-space prism of the individual, but carried the issue farther: what are the responses of society to this problem? If the location of day care centers is of major importance to women, how might they best be located so as to reduce the travel time required to reach them (Monk and Rengert 1982)? This is a problem in location-allocation, a branch of geography usually directed toward discovering the optimal location of industrial plants and similar

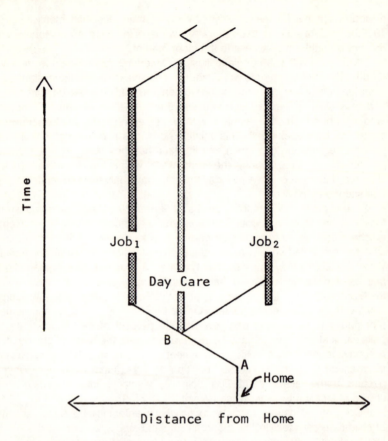

FIGURE 13   JANE'S TIME-SPACE PRISM. Jane, a hypothetical working mother, leaves home at time A, drives to the day care center, and drops off her child at time B. She might prefer Job₂, but she cannot reach it to begin work on time nor leave early enough to pick up her child. Thus she takes Job₁, which is located closer to the day care center (after Palm and Pred 1974; Figure 4).

economic enterprises. Only recently have geographers found location-allocation principles applicable to planning sites of social facilities — including day care centers. For example, L. Brown and colleagues examined a district in Columbus, Ohio, block by block, and were able to pinpoint the optimal location for future day care centers (Brown *et al.* 1972, 1974). Holmes and colleagues (1972) and Freestone (1977) examined the problem in an Australian context.

The pattern of women's daily travel behavior becomes clear. Women, especially those with young children, travel less than men. For women, travel is a greater burden. This applies to virtually all types of people, even criminals. Female criminals travel fewer miles to commit their crimes than male criminals (Ironically, however, when convicted, female criminals are sent to prisons farther from home than are males; G. Rengert 1975:17; G. Rengert and Monk 1982:8). Society as presently structured makes daily travel difficult for women. The case of Mildred Milovich is revealing. As a sales representative for a welding products company she traveled great distances and for long periods of time. Certainly this made her extraordinary compared with house-wives; even compared with other employed women her patterns of spatial activity were unusual. But her job would not be judged unusual for a man. Ms. Milovich arranged her trips so they could be tailored around the schedules of her two children. Notwithstand-ing, her non-traditional travel behavior cost her dearly: in a divorce case, her husband was awarded custody of the children because, as the Illinois judge ruled, "a stable environment" for children is more important than a woman being entitled to pursue a career of her choosing. The irony is that males apparently can become salesmen without disrupting the "stable environment" of the family. The message is that when women attempt to enter the man's world of work, society is often unable to accommo-date them and grant them the same degree of spatial mobility men have long enjoyed. Attitudes toward women and women's place in society are still controversial and slow to change. Women in the work force applaud those changes which have facilitated their economic equality, but still are unable to document many instances where they have been fully accepted.

Migration

In addition to the movement patterns reflecting day-to-day mobility are moves of longer duration. Factors which motivate a person to migrate are many, but the influences do not always operate equally on the two sexes. Some migration streams are dominated by women, some by men.

The influences involved in certain cases may be obvious. In the last century, for example, the movement from the settled East to the frontier West attracted far more men than women, so the sex ratio of that migration stream was quite high (male-dominated). On the other hand, the migrations from the rural East or from Europe to urban America were dominated by women seeking employment as domestic servants and as laborers in textile and other low-wage manufacturing firms. However, many generalizations about the sex selectivity of migration streams often are speculative and inconclusive. For example, a study of out-migration from Appalachia attempted to find socio-economic factors which explained the sex ratio of the migration stream. Most standard measures were unsatisfactory, and only the patterns of certain selected age groups could be explained with confidence (Peters 1976).

According to G. Trewartha (1969:138), "in the less developed countries migrants are predominatly male, whether the movement be international or intranational." This holds true for Africa and for Asia but not for Latin America. A survey of six Latin American countries revealed that fewer than 90 males migrated for each 100 females; in one country the sex ratio was 54 (A. Rengert 1981). The reason for the selectivity is the lack of opportunity for women in rural communities and the availability of jobs in the cities as domestic servants. Female migrants in Latin America come from poor, large families, whereas men come from smaller and wealthier families. This suggests that a well-off family may view the migration of a son to the city as an investment in the welfare of the total family because the son will send money home. Female migration is more an issue of her own economic survival (A. Rengert 1981:22; A. Rengert and J. Monk

1982b:3-4). In western Puerto Rico, however, Monk found that the economic motive (migration in order to find employment) was the rationale given for 64 percent of the males but only 19 percent of the females; some 54 percent of the females migrated in order to marry or to be with their husbands. Women, then were less likely than men to move independently of spouse or family (Monk 1981:40).

The patterns in Africa and Asia are complex. Domestic servants are not women but "houseboys," so unlike Latin America, women do not migrate to the cities to become domestics. Early in the colonial period, the migration stream was heavily dominated by males; women who migrated to work in towns were considered immoral and their occupations illegal (prostitution, the making of illegal beer). In 1911 Nairobi, for example, the sex ratio was 600 males per 100 females. Today the stream is still dominated by males, but more jobs are considered appropriate for females as well (Silberfein 1976). Today, women have begun to migrate in significant numbers to towns. Hence, the ratio of men to women is becoming more balanced (Strobel 1982:116).

In India, the sex ratio of the total migration stream in 1961 was 45 males per 100 females; however, the stream of persons migrating from one rural area to another rural area was heavily female: for each 100 females, only 31 males migrated. Rural-to-urban, urban-to-urban, and urban-to-rural streams collectively had a sex ratio of 102 (Gosal and Krishan 1975:199). The low sex ratio of the rural to rural stream has to do with the Indian marriage system. There is almost universal patrilocality (bride moves to groom's home), and marriages are endogamous (within one's own group). Often, however, marriage with partners in the same or nearby villages is considered incestuous. Thus there is a steady movement of young women from one village to another for the purpose of marriage. A single village is seen as the focus of a "bride-shed" (region from which brides are drawn). As a consequence of the incest taboo, this bride-shed is rather larger (so as to reach more potential partners) than theory might suggest (Libbee and Sopher 1975:347-59).

How far women migrate for the purpose of marriage compared with men varies from culture to culture. In India, far more married women than married men were born outside their present village of residence. The distance of marriage migration varies regionally in India, from under five miles (eight kilometers) to more than nineteen miles (thirty-one kilometers), with ten miles (sixteen kilometers) being average (Libbee and Sopher 1975:350-52; Mayfield 1972:393). In colonial Mexico, sex selectivity of distance to marriage was influenced by class: among non-Spanish groups, women migrated farther than men. Indian women, for example, migrated 25 percent farther than Indian men, but Spanish males and females traveled about the same distances (Yacher 1977:13). In colonial Massachusetts, sex differences overall were insignificant. Where a difference was found, the women traveled 28 percent farther than the men, 23 miles (37 kilometers) against 18 miles (29 kilometers; Kelly 1977). Among modern societies the distances understandably are greater. In 1972, women migrating to the Teton Valley of Idaho traveled an average of 185 miles (298 kilometers); men coming into the valley for marriage traveled 165 miles (266 kilometers; Green 1977).

In general, there does seem to be sex selectivity governing the distances that spouses travel for marriage. Brides apparently travel farther than grooms to the wedding site. This is a function of the greater prevalence to patrilocality (wife is expected to move to the husband's home) than matrilocality. Ironically, once married, women are more likely to migrate with husbands for employment purposes than vice versa.

Much has been said on female marriage migrations, the movements of women to be with husbands. The reverse situation also merits attention — movements of women to be free of husbands. Separation and divorce are traumatic for many reasons, among them being the change in residence for one or the other parties. In the U.S. when a marriage breaks up, both husband and wife charcteristically establish new households. In former times, the wife would return to her relatives. Families headed by women with children were rare. They still are rare today, comprising but 9.2 percent of all households, but the number of these families is growing; they increased 118 percent since 1960.

The pattern of the wife returning home to her family is fading in American society, but is still the rule in many non-Western societies. Among certain African groups when domestic disputes arise, the wife may return home, leaving the husband with domestic chores. This can be a powerful incentive for the man to make an extra effort to keep the family together because of the humiliation the man suffers from having to do "women's work." Muslim women in general are the most secluded and least mobile in Africa, but among the Islamic Hausa at least, the divorced woman gains a degree of status and freedom not available to married or never-married women. She is permitted to engage in retail enterprises and, thus, achieve spatial mobility and economic independence (Silberfein 1976).

The economic plight of divorced women is of concern world-wide, especially when children are involved. U.S. law rules that the father's responsibility to provide support for his children does not cease when the marriage dissolves. Although husband and wife may be spatially separated, contact is retained at least for financial purposes. Such ties are severed, of course, when one party simply disappears and cannot be found by the other. The runaway husband/father who vanishes and thus abrogates financial responsibility has long been common. A rather recent phenomenon, however, are the so-called "runaway wives." Women who flee their husbands, and often their children as well, have captured the attention of the media and public, in part because their numbers have increased dramatically in recent years. According to one source, in 1960 for every 300 husbands sought for abandoning a family, there was one wife who fled. However, by 1974 more wives than husbands were reported as having run away from the family environment (Sklar 1976:16-17). But even before 1960 the topic was of great interest to women, as Betty Friedan (1963:44) disclosed in her discussion of "togetherness," a fad of the 1950s which glorified the housewife role:

> In 1956 at the peak of togetherness, the bored editors of McCall's ran a little article called "The Mother Who Ran Away." To their amazement, it brought the highest readership of any article they had ever run. "It was our moment of truth," said a former editor. "We suddenly realized that all those women at home with their three and a half children were miserably unhappy."

Why would a woman run away from her family to desert the very institution which folklore and masculine rhetoric tells her should be her greatest source of fulfillment? Sklar studied runaway wives and indicated there are no easy answers applicable to all such women:

> Their complaints ranged from frustration because their husbands lived richer, fuller lives than they did and yet resented their wives' efforts to reach out to their own world, to complaints that their husbands had not lived up to their expectations, were poor providers, lousy fathers, and indifferent lovers (Sklar 1976:18).

Almost all saw marriage as tyranny and the source of the tyranny was the husband. The recent dramatic increase in the numbers of these women does not necessarily mean that husbands have suddenly become less suitable as mates than they were earlier. Rather, wives today, unlike their mothers and grandmothers, feel there are alternatives to remaining tied to a hopeless situation. Husbands have long considered abandonment as an option.

Where do runaway wives go? Obviously a great many destinations appeal to the large numbers of women, but Sklar suggests that Southern California dominated as a mecca for a disporportionately large number. Southern California holds the image of anonymity, prosperity, and the chance for a new beginning. For some, their new homes bring happiness. For many, though, guilt and further frustration follow them.

Divorced and separated wives make the decision to leave their husbands permanently or for an indefinite time to set up housekeeping in a new locale. Another type of movement-from-husband pattern is also characteristic of the spatial behavior of some women (but virtually no men): the traumatic flight of the wife who has been beaten by her husband. Violence toward a wife has always been present and often condoned. The comic-strip stereotype of the cave man knocking his mate senseless and dragging her to the cave is accepted uncritically as standard behavior for our ancestors. We might like to think that such an image, if indeed it had any validity at all, would only characterize our brutish forefathers. Recently, however, society has recognized that wife beating is epidemic among modern man as well. It does not merely occur in rare and bizarre circumstances, but is a common practice with only a few of the most extreme cases coming to the attention of authorities.

In terms of the spatial aspects of the issue, the movement of the abused wife commonly occurs as a spontaneous reaction to the husband's violence. Wife and kids hurriedly retreat to the nearest wife-abuse shelter, where their immediate physical and emotional needs are attended to. The shelters—inevitably far too few in number considering the need — act as secure havens where the husband cannot force his will upon the wife. Shelters are usually supported by charity, local government, or both; and they include a professional paid staff and often unpaid volunteers.

Friends and relatives, rather than formal shelters, often are the destinations of abused wives, and have functioned as such long before the shelter concept received concrete expression. The advantage the shelter has over friends and relatives, though, is that it may be unknown to, and unlocatable by, the husband. Surprisingly, tragically, friends and relatives often are powerless before an irate husband, and they even may side with him because of some notion that a woman belongs with her husband no matter what the consequences. The difficulties of a typical battered woman can partially be appreciated when one lists the events which occur in her life simultaneously: (1) she has been physically hurt, so she must nurse her painful bruises; (2) she has been emotionally hurt by a man whom presumably she cares for, or cared for; (3) she loses a house, to which she may have a considerable emotional attachment, and now must find new quarters; (4) she must comfort the kids who now may have to find new friends and new schools; and (5) she has no source of income so must begin immediately looking for a job. Few men will ever have to experience such a draining experience as this.

While considering the subject of violence toward women it is important to reflect on yet another facet of the problem — the forced migration of unwilling women from their homelands to new countries often under inhuman, barbaric circumstances. Slavery was a feature of European society from before Columbus's time and was widespread until the nineteenth century. Both women and men were violently ripped from their homes in Africa and sent to the Americas. Many more men than women were shipped from Africa, and within the U.S. too, the sex ratio of the slave trade overall was high. In the 15-19 year old bracket, however, the ratio was low, indicating the importance of young women for bearing new generations of slaves.

Less grotesque and less well known was the forced migration of white women from Britain and France to colonial America — convicted felons who left the harsh penal institutions of Europe to serve out their sentence in the colonies. Approximately a third of the felons thus transported were women, many of whom served their sentences, married, and became the foundation to which families today trace their colonial antecedents (Blumenthal 1962).

Forced migrations on the scale of the slave trade or felon relocations are from a former era. Yet a system of international terror and coercion does operate today, the female sexual slave trade. In the nineteenth century this was called "white slavery," based on a stereotype image of European women being sold into the harems and brothels of the Turks, Arabs, and other non-Western societies. Actually the pattern then as today involved women of all races in migration streams with origins and destinations from all over the world. The map (Figure 14) shows only a few streams: white women from Western Europe to Africa and the Middle East where Caucasian features are considered titillating; South American women to Mediterranean Europe and the Middle East; women from Southeast Asia to Europe. These are but a few; there are many more streams not mapped. This migration stream, unlike most outlined in these pages, is uniquely female. There is no corresponding selling of males for the purpose of perpetual rape (Barry 1979).

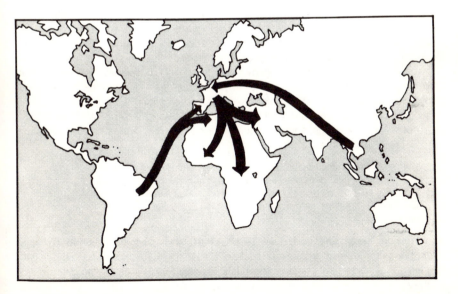

FIGURE 14   FEMALE SEXUAL SLAVERY MIGRATION ROUTES
(after information in Barry 1979).

Another migration stream affecting women only is the journey made to obtain an abortion. Monmonier and Williams (1973) attempted to find explanations for the nature of the migration stream of pregnant women into New York for the purpose of abortion in 1970-71, immediately before abortions were available nationwide. As would be expected, distance was the best indicator of the origin of the women (more women came from nearby states than from distant states), but when distance effects were removed, some regions contributed fewer, and others sent more women than would be expected. New England, the Middle West, and the Deep South sent fewer; the West sent more.

At the time of this writing the right to an abortion is being challenged by groups who oppose the practice. Should they be successful, feminists point out, abortions would become illegal in the United States. Because the demand for abortion is universal, migration streams would quickly develop: pregnant women flying to Europe, Japan, or to other countries so they would not be forced to bear an unwanted child. Only the rich could afford the luxury of a legal and safe abortion. Most of the journeys to abort would be poor women obtaining illegal and unsafe abortions close to home, just as they did before abortion became a right.

We conclude this discussion of female movement patterns with an examination of female migrant laborers. Female laborers have long been sought by employers because generally they are reliable and cheap. In many societies, however, women are discouraged, except under extreme circumstances, to leave home to find temporary work. In Japan, for example, rural women migrating to urban areas for seasonal jobs constitute only 8 percent of such migrants. Their numbers have increased greatly since World War II, however, because of economic necessity and because the family members left behind (especially grandparents rather than husbands) are willing to take on parental responsibilities (Oshiro 1978:1982).

The female migrant laborer presents an interesting case study in point of view. Lee Seymour views the female migrant as participating unwittingly in an exploitive system. The female migrants earn a low wage (because they are migrants, because they often are from minority races, and because they are female). Their low wage depresses the wage level for all workers. Seymour finds here a lesson for the working class to unite, to do away with its racial and sexual biases, and thereby to improve conditions generally (Seymour 1976). However, in a study of migration of Turkish women, one author observed that female workers became "emancipated" as a result of the move. Compared with women who did not migrate, or with male migrants, they became more "now-oriented" and concerned with their personal welfare. They put relatively little of their earnings into savings, and they were far less likely than men to send money back to their families in Turkey:

> It appears that women not only look upon a stay abroad as a better opportunity to work, or better said, the only permissible place to work and save, but also to enjoy a different life style. This is traceable in their outspoken preference for traveling as fun, a tendency not noticeable among men (Abadan-Unat 1977:45).

Their greater independent behavior results from relative economic independence, even though their actual wages may be low. The conclusions expressed in these two studies are not necessarily incompatible. It is possible that European employers, even as they pay non-European females a paltry wage, are improving the women's status relative to men and to other women at home.

Women's Movement

The movement patterns of women differ from those of men, both for short term travel and long term migrations. Many of these differences reveal the repressive nature of contemporary society. Over and over we observe sex selectivity in movement patterns operating to the males' advantage. Of course this not inevitably the case; probably most types of human movements affect the two sexes equally, and some discriminate against men. As noted in the case of the slave trade, for example, being male was a disadvantage for most age groups. Another type of movement which is sex selective to the detriment of males is mobilization for war. In war everyone loses, but men suffer greater physical hardship than women.

The general pattern, however, is that women travel less than men and suffer as a result of this disparity. This reduced travel reflects the fact that the world of women has restricted dimensions compared with the man's world. Women thus miss much of the excitement and stimulation which travel implies. This theme, among others, is examined in the next chapter.

3

What Does She Think?

In recent years, interest in the environment and in people's attitudes toward the environment has stimulated a geographical concern with 'environmental perception.' Essentially this field attempts to understand how humans learn about and behave in the space which surrounds them.

Sex Differences in Environmental Perception

Psychologically, individuals live at the center of their own, unique personal worlds. The space of that world stretches out endlessly from the position of the individual. In that world are found the places which the individual knows and finds important: the home, house of friends, distant towns — a whole personalized atlas of places to which the individual can relate. The places in a subjective world are known in an objective manner, but they are evaluated subjectively as well. The individual feels certain ways about some parts of his or her world, but feels differently about other parts of that environment. This influences what an individual will remember from an environment. Meaningful places will be remembered, others may not.

The meaning each individual attaches to a personal universe is unique, but there is a degree of communality among members of a group. Old people find certain places meaningful which would bore teenagers. The world of the rich contains places which are denied to the poor. Gender difference also influences how our personal worlds are structured. Yi-Fu Tuan discusses this, as related to a married couple:

> On a shopping expedition the man and woman will want to look into different stores. They may walk arm in arm but they do not thereby see and hear the same things. Occasionally they are jolted out of their own perceptual world to make a courtesy call on that of another, as, for example, when the husband asks his wife to admire some golf clubs in the shop window (Tuan 1974:62).

Individuals know the places near home the best, and this familiarity is comforting. We like to have a secure base upon which we can establish a foundation. This is home, the "hearth." As we saw in Chapter 2, women do less traveling away from home than men, and spend more time at home. What does this mean in terms of our "mental maps," our mental image of our personal world? Do women stay at home because to them, home is a more enjoyable place than far-from-home places? The familiar adage, "a woman's place is in the home," seems to suggest this. The English writer, Lord Raglan, says that the indoor space of the home is proper for a woman, especially a married woman, but not the outdoors: "Indoors a married woman is mistress. . . . In her house she has, that is to say, a kind of sanctity which she loses as soon as she goes out of doors" (Raglan 1964:41).

This traditional, stereotyped view of the role of women and their personal worlds can be summarized thus: the woman, especially when she is wife and mother, spends most of her time in the house in order to provide a pleasant environment for husband and children. Her role may confine her to the house and places nearby, but she receives greatest joys from those activities which center on the home. Places away from the house, on the other hand, may not be appropriate for her to visit, not without her husband or at least not without other women. The farther a place is from home, the less attraction it would hold for her. Places far from home may in fact be dangerous.

Unfamiliar landscapes do hold dangers, to be sure, not only for women but for men as well. Hooligans, wild animals, and possible natural disasters have the potential to cause grave bodily harm. In the Greek classic *The Odyssey,* Ulysses (Odysseus) continually encountered dangers which all but destroyed him and his crew. For example, while passing the lair of the Sirens, Ulysses cleverly plugged the ears of the sailors so they could not hear the Siren's enticingly beautiful songs which would have lured them onto the rocks and destruction. Without this precaution, their journey would have ended in tragedy. Today, the word "jungle" conveys more than a picture of lush tropical vegetation. It also suggests a distant place which is unfamiliar and dangerous to the unwary. Men and women alilke are susceptible to distant dangers, but popular widsom tells us that men are better able to cope, perhaps because of superior speed and muscle strength, or perhaps because of a more aggressive personality.

The traditional argument that women belong in the home needs to be addressed. First, however, we examine the real difficulties which confront women in the world outside the home, especially when traveling far distances alone.

Anxiety Away from Home

In contemporary society there are a number of barriers which prevent women from traveling with as much freedom as men. Many of these are major considerations not to be taken lightly, some are less fundamental.

Travel in modern society requires that complex pieces of machinery function properly. When they fail, the traveler is inconvenienced, frustrated, or, worse, endangered. The private automobile can be a source of gratification for the freedom it affords, but breakdowns are nagging sources of anxiety. In the traditional development of girls and boys, boys are more likely than girls to receive some basic training in emergency auto repair. Women are taught to depend on men for solutions to mechanical problems, and by and large women suffer more from anxiety of possible car failure than men. To help the modern woman feel comfortable with her automobile, the popular media provide help guides directed toward women. For example, *Ms. Magazine* occasionally runs a feature called "Populist Mechanics" which provides both practical advice on mechanics as well as encouragement for women to try to familiarize themselves with the basics of machinery.

Then there is the matter of overnight stays in distant towns. Imagine, for example, a salesperson staying at a hotel. After checking in, the person has dinner alone in the dining room, then perhaps a drink at the bar before retiring. If the person is male this causes no particular difficulty, but if the person is a woman, she may run into embarrassing situations. Hotel clerks rarely encounter unaccompanied women (though they are less remarkable today than in the past). Travel writer Judith Hennessee says, "The room clerk calls you 'honey' and thinks maybe you're a hooker in disguise." At dinner, and more so at the bar, the solo woman may be approached by attentive males. Some women handle such situations easily, but others prefer simply to skip dinner or to snack in their rooms rather than constantly be subjected to pickup hassles (Hennessee 1981:38). This example, as with others, illustrates that women have a more constricted spatial environment than men.

The problem of unwanted and unreciprocated attentions by the opposite sex — sexual harassment — is larger and more serious than most people, men especially, are aware. Both sexes are guilty of harassing, but by far the greatest offenders are men. Harassment takes many forms and occurs in many places. In the workplace, male managers hug, pat, caress, squeeze, and otherwise violate the privacy of female employees. In universities professors intimidate students with unsolicited overtures of intimacy. In large part, harassment such as this reflects the pervasive man-superior, woman-inferior role structure of society.

Power differences based on gender are manifested in many ways. Men touch women more often than women touch men, for example. Men call women by their first names sooner than women do. Studies in France show that men use the familiar "tu" form of "you" when women would feel more comfortable with the formal "vous." Men addressing children, pets, and women communicate both verbally and non-verbally that they see themselves as superior (Parlee 1975:137).

A degrading form of harassment, which unfortunately and incorrectly is dismissed as innocuous flirtation, is street hassling. This form of invasion of privacy, more common abroad than in the United States, is a frequent complaint, especially of female American tourists who have been accosted by the groping hands of men in the streets of foreign countries. A study by Van Gelder (1981) revealed that the problem is most severe in "the macho Mediterranean" and Latin countries generally: Mexico, France, Spain, Greece, and Middle East, and most notoriously, Italy. She and her informants report being grabbed, pinched, hugged, and generally subjected to the repulsive stroking hands of strange men. Bernard and Schlaffer (1981) attempted to find out why men harass women who are simply going about their business, not "asking for it":

> Pressed for an explanation of their behavior, most of the men initially were at a loss. It alleviates boredom, it gives them a feeling of youthful camaraderie when they discuss women with other men; it's "fun" and it "doesn't hurt anybody," they often added a little defensively. The notion that women dislike this was a novel idea for most men . . .

Street hassling is pernicious because it may seem at first glance to be trivial, harmless, even complimentary. But most women find it an offensive infringement of their right to personal integrity. The effect on environmental perception is that streets, sidewalks, and other spaces where men roam freely become zones of hostile space for women.

Bernard and Schlaffer found the street hasslers by and large did not see their act as assault. They acted without thinking. However, some 15 percent of the men interviewed reported they deliberately wanted to anger or humiliate the victim. This expression of aggression and violence brings up the much more serious attack on female personal integrity: rape.

The role played by the crime of rape to oppress women can hardly be overstated. Rape has devastating effects on individual women who are victims, and in broader ways it intimidates all women: all classes of women, all age groups, all races, women of all regions — all females are potential rape victims. In a chilling report, Allen Johnson examines statistics of completed or attempted rapes in the United States, and concludes that nationally, "a *conservative* estimate is that, under current conditions, 20-30 percent of girls now twelve years old will suffer a violent sexual attack during the remainder of their lives." He stresses that sexual aggression is of major importance: the average woman, he says, "is just as likely to suffer a sexual attack as she is to be diagnosed as having cancer, or to experience a divorce. Yet, these events receive considerably more attention than does sexual assault" (Johnson 1980:145-6). Edward Shorter (1977) reported the following statistics on rapes per 100,000 female population from the early 1970s: Italy 5.4; Australia 8.7; Canada 13.2; West Germany 21.6; and the United States 44.4. Clearly, rape is a major crime and, sadly, the United States is a world leader.

Where do rapes take place? The question is difficult to answer definitively because statistics are gathered from police reports of hundreds of counties and cities, and standardization of terminology is lacking. One approach is to investigate the characteristics of the districts where rapes tend to occur. Areas adjacent to the central business districts of towns are high crime areas generally, and rape zones specifically. Areas of poor street lighting, areas where citizen or police surveillance is weak, and areas which have a large number of vacant dwellings are frequently chosen by the rapist. Likewise, city districts where young women constitute a high percentage of the population, districts with a high population density generally, and where socio-economic conditions are below standard have higher than average rape reports (Beard 1978:6-20).

Figure 15 shows the locations of 284 reported rapes in Broward County, Florida, a suburb of Miami. The percentages shown are probably typical of comparable figures from other localities (Harries 1974). Whatever the breakdown may be for a given community, and there seems to be major differences place to place, one issue is clear: no place is safe. Rapes are not merely brutal acts taking place in the seamy quarters of a community. They may occur any place, any time. Even the woman's home, that symbol of traditional feminine safety and security, is a dangerous place. If one believes that "a woman's place is in the home," one should also recognize that the rapist often follows the same philosophy.

What effect does rape have on the environmental image which women construct mentally? How does rape affect environmental perception? Clearly fear of rape, in hand with the perceived physical disadvantage women have compared with men in terms of speed and muscle strength, causes women to be more apprehensive about parts of their environment than men. In a study of six neighborhoods of three American cities, Gordon and colleagues (1980:S147) found that 49 percent of women in their sample indicated that they felt "very unsafe" or "somewhat unsafe" when out alone in their neighborhoods at night; only 7.5 percent of the men responded in this way. The answers of women to questions about their spatial behavior revealed the importance of fear in their lives. When asked, how frequently do you walk in the neighborhood alone after dark, a quarter of the women (but only 3 percent of the men) responded they never

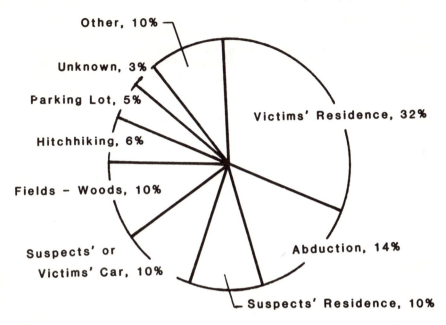

FIGURE 15 LOCATION OF RAPE IN BROWARD COUNTY, FLORIDA, 1977-78 (Broward County Human Relations Division, Women's Concerns Section 1978).

did this activity. Nearly half of the women (8 percent of the men) say they never go downtown alone after dark. Public transportation, upon which women are more dependent than men, is never used at night by nearly half of the women respondents compared with 29 percent of the men. Jeanne Fagnani likewise showed that public transportation is feared by women of Paris. Women who lack private automobiles are disadvantaged, and are reluctant to ride the metro (subway): "the metro is a closed place, not open to the exterior, without possible escape from the insistent, indiscreet glances directed [toward women] by certain men" (Fagnani 1977:558).

Women's concern for crime is greater than men's even though for most crimes women are victimized less frequently than men. In large part this reaction to crime results from their specific physical attack. The mental maps of women reflect this fear. Places which men may frequent are denied to women, not only traditionally all-male hangouts like bars, but downtown areas, parks, transportation facilities and other public areas. The fear of rape, says Susan Griffin (in Gordon *et al.* 1980:S145), "keeps women off the streets at night. Keeps women at home. Keeps women modest for fear that they be thought provocative." Because women perceive dangers in places men find safe, women are not only victims of sexual aggression, they are also victims of foregone opportunities to explore a larger environment.

Unquestionably travel away from the home and the neighborhood can prove stressful because of the discomforts and dangers of unfamiliar environments. It is not surprising that millions of people, women and men alike, suffer anxiety when venturing beyond their familiar neighborhood routes. In fact the mental disorder agoraphobia, fear of open places, afflicts as many as 2.5 million Americans. It may be the most common of the phobias. Agoraphobiacs, when exposed to unfamiliar places, have panic attacks with weakness of legs, shortness of breath, heart palpitations, and general disorientation. Rather than expose themselves to stressful surroundings, many agoraphobiacs simply remain in the house as much as possible. Agoraphobia is found in all geographic regions of the country and among all social classes. But of particular interest, some 85 to 90 percent of the sufferers are women (*Time* 1977b; Washburne and Chambless 1978).

What causes the illness, how it should be treated, and why it overwhelmingly afflicts women are questions which are open to debate. Specialists are divided. A few feel it results from hormonal imbalances. Freudians suggest the cause is repressed sexual urges during childhood. Feminist therapists, however, see agoraphobia as reflecting "the reality of women's isolation and poor self-image." They believe women suffer because they are taught as girls that the world outside is dangerous. Such women grow to be stay-at-home housewives who are able to reject the outdoors and can afford to nurse these fears of the unknown. Given confidence and opportunities of employment, feminists contend, women will suffer no more from agoraphobia than do men (*Time* 1977b; Fox 1977:814).

Most women, of course, are not agoraphobiacs. But Colette Dowling (1981) thinks women secretly yearn to be taken care of and fear autonomy. Women depend upon men for support when engaged in matters outside the home — or at least they would like to be dependent. Feminists do not identify with this ideology because feminism encourages self-reliance for women. Yet millions of women have been raised to view men as important, perhaps indispensible personal support systems. But men, too, are dependent. Throughout their lives they depend on one woman or another for care and comfort. They may actually be the more dependent sex, the popular image to the contrary notwithstanding. It is a human tendency, not a uniquely female or male trait, to long to be cared for (Mead 1981).

For both sexes, home serves as a powerful symbol as a safe locale in a troubled world, a haven where we are loved, and where the dangers of the outside world may not intrude. A man's home is his castle; we should like to think it a fortress for women as well. Rapes and violence in the home taint the image of home-as-bastion, but notwithstanding, the solid symbol of the home as a secure place endures. As the fear of crime data show, women find home far more secure than the world outside.

Agreeable Strangeness of Distant Places

In spite of the dangers, the anxieties and the inconveniences, the world outside our home and neighborhood can conjure positive images as well, what Philip Wagner (1972:47) called "an agreeable sense of strangeness" of new environments (see also Tuan 1973). Distant places are stimulating, exciting, alluring. Near space is better known to us, but the "variety and intensity of experience increase with distance. The further we are from home, the more unusual and stimulating the events we encounter" (Abler *et al.* 1971:9, Figure 1-6). Wanderlust beckons us to face the dangers of travel in order to experience firsthand the pleasures of foreign places. Ulysses, mindful of the dangers, wanted so badly to hear the Sirens' songs that he lashed himself to the mast of his ship so he would not be able to steer a course to destruction. Each of us is a Ulysses who yearns to explore new lands, to investigate *terra incognita* (Wright 1947).

We are ambivalent, then, about distant places. We are attracted to them, yet we may view travel with a sense of awe, even fear. For most people, though, the attractions outweigh the inconveniences. In a survey of its readers, *Psychology Today* found that the ideal vacation overwhelmingly featured some sort of travel away from home; only 13 percent of the respondents favored stay-at-home activities such as using the time to do creative projects or to be with family (Rubenstein 1980:72).

Moreover, the symbol of home is an ambiguous one too. Home may evoke positive images such as security, comfort, and warmth. We enjoy the positive sensations associated with home, but not always do we recognize that the negative aspects may disturb us. Here is where sex differences play a major role. Tognoli (1979, p. 601, 604) says "There is a separation of roles for many adult males and females in relation to the home, resulting in an outside/inside dichotomy." Women (more than men) tend to see the home as an expression of the personal identities, whereas men feel comfortable socializing, not so much in the home as in offices, bars, bowling alleys and stadiums. Men are generally more ambivalent toward the home than women are, yet for both sexes the attitude is not easily recognized or articulated. It is indicative, for example, that in the mental health profession we have a name for fear of places outside the home (agoraphobia) but there is no "domestaphobia" or some such — fear or rejection of one's home.

For women it is especially hard to recognize and find expression for these feelings of ambivalence. One of the most influential of feminist books, *The Feminist Mystique* by Betty Friedan, uses this theme as a starting point. In her first chapter, entitled "The Problem Which Has No Name," she talks about the convention of women staying at home. The attitudes of the late 1940s and 50s were that women, who previously had been employed in the defense plants of World War II, were expected to, and in fact did, give up their jobs to men and return to the kitchen. On the surface women seemed to accept being homebound. Gradually, though, more and more women experienced a general malaise which they could not even name; that is, they could not easily articulate their difficulties, even to themselves (Friedan 1963).

The problem (or a major part, at least) was that they found domestic isolation stifling and wanted the stimulation of experiencing places beyond the house. They listened to the proposition that fulfillment would be found only if they married, had children, worked hard and kept the house tidy, kept the laundry "cleaner than clean" (a senseless claim of a detergent of the time), and left worldly matters to men. They listened but found it harder and harder to accept. For one thing, if homemaking and child minding were indeed fulfilling and creative, then surely they would be such for both sexes. Yet overwhelmingly women, not men, garnered the pleasures of such activities. Either men were being cheated out of their share of the joy of domestic creativity, or such "joys" were largely blown out of proportion to the reality of domestic life. Whichever way one reads it, one sex or the other was being cheated. Since the number of women in the labor force has steadily risen, one could conclude that they considered themselves to be the cheated sex.

Not only feminists, but increasingly more women who do not necessarily think of themselves as feminists, feel women are the ones who are losing out. Wilma Scott Heide (1973), former President of the National Organization for Women, condemns "the ghetto of one's home," and rejects the "housewife syndrome," saying "I do not accept that anyone can marry a house." Male feminist Warren Ferrell (1975:164) points out the sad irony that men want women to remain in the housewife role, but at the same time they will demonstrate disrespect of women for being overly concerned with domestic affairs. Betty Friedan rejects the attempts made by non-feminist traditionalists who contend that housework is wonderfully creative if only the woman views it as such. Friedan says:

> Love and children and home are good, but they are not the whole world. . . . Why should women try to make housework "something more," instead of moving on the frontiers of their own time, as American women moved beside their husbands on the old frontiers? (Friedan 1963:60)

Moreover, the home is not as safe an environment as one might suppose. Most accidents occur in the home. Rape statistics, mentioned above, are likewise alarming: most rapes occur in private homes. Many of these are by men whom the woman knew and trusted, but many others are strangers who somehow gain entry into the house. In either event, the home is less of a secure fortress than one might think. Isolating a woman indoors does not insure her safety.

Yet the prevailing division of labor secludes women to the home environment. What do women think about, vis-a-vis the indoor space of home as opposed to the outdoor space of the world? Probably no direct studies have been done on this topic, but some surrogate measures are of interest.

One source of information may be the types of literature read by the two sexes. Take, for example, the romantic novels. In this group we include the gothics, the historical romances (*Gone with the Wind* was, perhaps, the most substantial and most successful of these) and more recently the "contemporaries," which place the woman heroine in a modern setting but otherwise are of the same *genre*. All of these are written primarily by women for a female audience. The market for such novels is tremendous and all major paperback publishing houses put out a steady supply. According to *The Wall Street Journal,* these romances "have become publishing's answer to the Big Mac: They are juicy, cheap, predictable and devoured in stupefying quantities by legions of loyal fans" (Grover 1980). That women buy such books obviously suggests that when housework permits, these novels stimulate females to reflect on settings and situations beyond the confines of the home. Of particular interest to geographers is the role of distant settings. The editor of one popular house (Gallen Books) says "The core fantasy is wealth, power, clothes, travel and a glorious career" (Sullivan 1981). A successful author, Diana Haviland, says the formula for creating a successful romance includes exposing the reader to a succession of exotic locales. "The heroines move about so much they practically live out of suitcases. Their love affairs are almost always consummated on ships or in hotels" (Grover 1980). These romances are not guidebooks to feminist enlightenment by any means. They are modeled more on Cinderella and Sleeping Beauty than Wonder Woman. The heroine relies heavily on male support, and needs an older, dominant (though sensitive) man to help her out of who-knows-what situations.

Fantasizing about distant locales is by no means an exclusively female hobby. War novels, westerns, and science fiction, which appeal to men, employ distant locales as settings. But 70 percent of fiction readers are women (Grover 1980), and it is apparent that women vicariously enjoy thoughts of adventure in distant places. We might realistically suggest, however, that exotic locales in romantic fiction are employed less for their inherent qualities, such as landscape beauty or cultural stimulation, than for their value as plausible settings where interpersonal relationships can unfold. The point of having the heroine travel is not for geographical enlightenment so much as to put her in a position where she can make a new male acquaintance. Similarly, in disaster novels (fiction centered on massive natural or human-made disasters such as hurricanes or floods) the main male characters are scientists or journalists battling to save humanity, whereas the female figures pay less attention to awesome nature than to the men in the stories, with whom they inevitably fall in love (Liverman and Sherman 1981). Indeed, physical space and objects in it (mountains, rivers) often serve as metaphors and symbols rather than what they are in reality. Drawing from an unpublished study, Zelinsky and collaborators (1982) said:

> Burton (1976) has explored women's perceptions of country and city landscapes through analysis of North American novels by and about women. She shows their perceptions of the physical and social landscape to be shaped by conflicts between the needs for family relationships and for personal scope and freedom. In the novels analysed, it is not unusual to find journeys between city and county serving as metaphors for personal explorations and attempts to improve social and physical settings.

Whatever role women, men, and landscape may play in fiction, it is clear that the distant setting is important. Novels set in the kitchen seem to have little appeal to either sex.

Then there is the matter of vacation preferences. The *Psychology Today* study of vacations showed that women, more than men, rate highest those vacations which would make them carefree, adventurous, and daring. Men, on the other hand, "prefer the security of revisiting familiar places rather than the excitement of discovering new ones." Men enjoy vacations less than women, and are more eager to return to work after vacations. Though both women and men rate stay-at-home vacations low, men were more enthusiastic about them than women (16 percent vs. 12 percent) (Rubenstein 1980:63, 72).

The work done by geographers seems to suggest that there are sex-linked (or, more properly, *gender-linked*) differences in the formation of environmental images, but little is known on how much one sex reflects upon near-by places as opposed to distant ones. J. D. Porteous (1976:386), for example, says, "Recent cognitive mapping studies have shown that, excluding downtown areas that are known to almost everyone, cognitive maps are most detailed in the region of the home. This is especially true for women. . . ." His contention is intriguing, but would be more convincing if it were based on a larger set of experiential studies. Other indicators suggest the opposite. For example, our preliminary analysis of the content of mental maps drawn by university students suggests that if anything, the mental maps made by female students of their personal worlds contain more distant and exotic places than maps drawn by men. Clearly here is an area which warrants more study.

Women enjoy travel, but their tastes vary regarding traveling companions. Some women prefer or require a man to be present. Many wives, for example, would not think of vacationing without their husbands. Other women vacation alone — or at least start out alone — but find men en route. A single woman may design her vacation with the strong possibility that she might develop a friendship with a new man. For such women the notion of adventure and excitement might closely conform to the stereotypes coming from the popular media: ocean voyages on a "Love Boat," or escapes to a "Fantasy Island." In dream vacations such as these, men play an important, perhaps indispensable role. Falling in love, even marriage, might seem wonderfully romantic but not totally unrealistic. Failure to meet at least one pleasant male would prove the entire vacation a failure. Again, as with the role of setting in fiction, the exotic landscapes of romantic holidays such as these become little more than background for the real action in the personal drama: love, romance, passion. In all cases the women portray a dependent role.

Women traveling with men or to find men have well established traditions. Far fewer are women who travel alone or with other women for the sake of appreciating the inherent qualities of the distant locale. Numerous women travelers, explorers, and adventurers from earlier periods come to mind: daring women who spend years in uncharted realms, often suffering tremendous hardships. Homer in fact, the writer of the Greek epic Ulysses, may actually have been a woman (Fowles 1980:51). Today travel is usually easier. Feminist travel agents can provide female clients a variety of options. For example, a 1980 special in *Ms. Magazine* listed scores of tours, conferences, retreats, spas, and resorts catering to women without men. Specific attractions varied, but common to all was privacy or the opportunity to meet other women (Sweet 1980).

Some women design their own solo adventures. Claudia Dreyfus (1980) related experiences of unaccompanied travel in Africa. Her narrative includes a list of "do's and don'ts" which help the solo woman avoid the hassles women find so annoying. At times Dreyfus was lonely, sometimes she received poor treatment. However, she reports, "It was the best thing I ever did for myself. In solo traveling, I had no support system like the one I had back home; for three months I had to be everything for myself." By herself on the slopes of Mt. Kilimanjaro she found courage. Equally if not more courageous was Naomi James, who in 1977 sailed single-handed around the world, breaking the record for speed. Her 30,000 mile (48,279 kilometer) nine-month journey was a constant fight for survival. "When you're fighting to survive," she discovered from her experience, "you're not afraid anymore" (James 1979).

Intrepid though they may wish to be, many solo women lack the resources to tour remote places like highland East Africa. Family responsibilities restrict some. The experience of Annie Dillard (1974) may interest such women. Dillard spent a year being in, and becoming part of, the natural environment. For her the journey was not to a landscape distant in space. In fact it was to her own wilderness neighborhood, a small but wild tract in the Blue Ridge Mountains of Virginia. She immersed herself in the dynamic flow of nature. Unobtrusively she became a part of the landscape. She would lie in the grass for hours, simply observing. More poet than scientist, she would fall to sensations of great rapture, for example while watching mockingbirds and butterflies. Terror too would strike: watching a copperhead snake, or witnessing a water bug suck the body of a frog from its skin. Nature, even close to home, can comfort yet horrify.

Dillard's journey to wilderness took place on a day to day basis. Some women spend long periods in the wilds. Such journeys once were considered inappropriate for women. Wilderness was man's realm. But in recent years this has changed. Women are living, working, and playing in the wilderness in increasing numbers. The way has been charted by pathfinders, women who show other women places formerly thought too dangerous. China Galland is one such leader. Her book *Women in the Wilderness* (Galland 1980) recounts all-women adventures: rafting down the Colorado River, kayak sailing in the Gulf of California, mountain climbing in the Himalayas. Ann LaBastille's book (1980), with an almost identical title *(Women and Wilderness)* relates life stories of women in wilderness professions. The dangers of travel to isolated locations are discussed, including the danger of rape. Both women conclude that with proper training and respect for the difficulties, women can find exhilaration and enrichment from the beauties of the natural environment.

Wilderness recreation travel is open to women in large numbers; professional exploration, however, is available to very few of either sex. The exploits of one explorer, however, bear mentioning. In 1979, Sylvia Earle made the deepest dive made by any human in a diving suit when she was lowered to a depth of 1250 feet (381 meters) in the waters off Hawaii (Bollet, 1981). For her accomplishment she was voted (by the narrowest of margins) membership in the previously all male Explorers Club.

The ultimate travel experience in the minds of many takes the voyager not merely to exotic earthly environments but to the very reaches of space itself. The flights of astronauts, with but three exceptions, have been male-only enterprises. Women as astronauts have had an inglorious career by and large. According to the National Aeronautics and Space Administration (NASA), two of the nineteen candidates (11 percent) selected to receive astronaut training in July, 1980, were women. This percentage was down somewhat from the six of thirty-six (17 percent) selected two years earlier; these six NASA called "the first women astronauts." However, as early as 1959 women were being considered for the astronaut program. Thirteen women had gone through initial testing and training, then were swept aside for reasons unknown. Not, apparently, because they were unsuited:

> In the opinion of the scientists evaluating the test results, women were as capable and as suitable as men for space flight; in some ways, more suitable. For instance, women, on an average, weighed less and consumed less food and oxygen — no small consideration when the cost of putting anything (animal, mineral, or vegetable) into space was assessed at approximately $1,000 per pound (McCullough 1973:43).

The ultimate travel experience, the journey beyond earth's atmosphere, remained the privilege of an all-male club, at least until recently for Americans, but in June, 1963, the Soviet Union sent Valentina Tereshkova into space. NASA officials dismissed her accomplishment as "a publicity stunt" (McCullough 1973:45). It was not until August of 1982 that the second female flew in space, again a Russian: Cosmonaut Svetlana Savitskaya. America's females had not had similar opportunities, but at least American women were now being admitted for astronaut training. The first American woman in space, Sally Ride, was among the Space Shuttle crew in April, 1983. Finally, American girls can dream that they themselves may someday venture into space.

Innate Abilities

The issue of the female astronauts raises an interesting question: Why was it that in the early days of the program women were not accepted for astronaut training? Though NASA did not explain its early reluctance, one possibility is that women inherently lack certain required traits that men possess. Test results refuted this, but perhaps officials reasoned (as people commonly do) that their female psychological make-up automatically should exclude them. Phrasing this argument more broadly, many people of both sexes contend that when women attempt to integrate formerly all-male professions, such as astronaut, they are going 'against their nature.' They are attempting to accomplish tasks for which they are essentially and fundamentally unsuited. Ultimately this will result in frustration — as a five-foot basketball player would experience trying to become a professional. The argument contends that, after all, there are differences between the sexes. (Often this particular revelation is accompanied by supposedly insightful snickers.) The differences are not merely differences of physiology, but mental and emotional ones as well. Men are "naturally" more suited for the outdoors, for travel, for all tasks requiring an aggressive composure and lots of muscle; on the other hand, men avoid domestic drudgery and such tasks. The current division of labor, the argument continues, is just and proper because over the eons specialization of tasks resulted from natural abilities. An anti-ERA bumper sticker seen on automobiles in the 1970s summed up the position with an apparently simple phrase, "Stop ERA — You Can't Fool Mother Nature."

Feminists, one might well imagine, have much to criticize in this argument. On some points there is agreement, however. Women are indeed "different." Some differences related to the reproductive function are undisputed: women bear and nurse children, men cannot. For virtually all other differences, however, one must use qualifiers and speak of general tendencies and averages rather than absolutes. Most men possess greater upper body strength, weigh more, are taller, and run faster than most women. These characteristics can be tested for large populations, and the findings are matters of fact which are rarely questioned. However, this implies *nothing* when comparing individuals. With social behavior, there is difficulty even in agreeing whether there are differences, let alone how any supposed differences arose. Concerning sex differences in behavior, Wrightman and Deaux (1981:408) say that "the areas which comparisons could be made are as numerous as the chapters in a book." They examine three areas briefly: aggression (women are thought less aggressive than men); conformity (women are thought to be more conforming and persuadable than men); and motivation for achievement (men are thought to have higher levels of motivation to achieve success than women). They point out that in these and most other areas, no simple answers can be given to explain sex differences. Are men more aggressive? Many researchers say yes, overall, but in certain situations women seem to display greater levels of aggression than men.

The important point with respect to sex differences in behavior is to recognize that for most behaviors it is extremely difficult, often impossible, to determine whether the observed differences result from inherent, biologically based traits, or are the result of training and conditioning. Even within the first few hours of birth, girl babies are treated differently from boy babies (Vaughter 1976:124); we expect newborns to conform right from the start to the gender roles laid down by society. Differences which are truly inherent cannot be altered at will. Men, for example, cannot be "trained" to give birth. Motherhood always and without exception will be denied to men. But what types of behavior are so rigid and irrefutably sex-based as this? Hardly any, perhaps none.

Take, for example, the matter, not of biological motherhood, but of "maternal instinct," the supposed tendency for mothers naturally and innately to love, care for, and protect their offspring. A sacred institution is motherhood in our society, but is motherly love "innate?" Or is it merely the expected behavior, the societal norms of the moment? Could love of children merely result from careful training and not from innate drives? Evidence suggests the former, in fact. In some groups, the Ik of East Africa, for example, mothers supposedly abandon their children and display no signs of affection or protectiveness. The Yanomano of Brazil apparently will selectively let children starve to death (M. Harris 1978:90-92). In European society too, the "maternal instinct" is a recent phenomenon. According to French scholar Elisabeth Badinter, it is just a myth, invented 200 years ago to subjugate women. She cites sobering evidence that suggests that mothers treated children then in a manner we would call brutal today (Badinter 1981; Leo, 1980; Lorber *et al.* 1981). If Badinter is correct, if "maternal instinct" is not instinct at all but learned behavior, then such behavior can be learned by men as well as by women. Men, denied by biology the ability to bear children, can with training become as adept at loving, nurturing, and caring for children as women. Men can take comfort in the potential expansion of their roles.

Recalling the theme of this chapter, environmental perception, we may question whether the sex differences in environmental images noted above are truly innate or simply learned. Feminists might prefer to dismiss such differences as the products of differential upbringing, boys taught and encouraged to reflect upon and attend to outdoor space (the public sphere), girls directed to relate well to personal body space and to interiors (the domestic sphere). The psychologist Eric Erickson, who studied children at play, noted the tendency for the sexes to attend to space types in this manner. But Erickson has been questioned, refuted, even satirized, and his experiments convinced feminists of nothing relating to innate qualities in girls and boys. However, the recent research on "spatial abilities" shows rather convincingly that even at early ages, females score lower on tests of spatial organization (perception of objects in space) and spatial visualization (the ability to imagine movements of objects in space; L. Harris 1979:135). Harris cites tests which confirm these findings, including sense of direction tests, maze problems, pattern walking, map reading, tracking, geographical knowledge, and numerous others (L. Harris 1978:405-522).

Some researchers find definite implications in the studies on spatial abilities. Robert and Ruth Munroe (1971:22), for example, noted that among the Logoli of East Africa, "male children were more skillful than Logoli female children at certain tests requiring the capacity to perform a set of behaviors ordered sequentially in space." These results, and other information on spatial abilities, lead them to conclude that: "it is therefore not surprising to find males so disproportionately represented in such fields as the physical sciences, engineering, and architecture, where spatial ability is an important element in successful performance." Likewise, geographer Wolf Roder (1977) concluded that differences in 'geographical abilities' in women and men appear to be biologically based, and even if we eliminate 'social discrimination against women' we would never be able to recruit as many women as men into the field because, he contends, of 'biological differences' which favor men over women.

If the acknowledged differences in spatial abilities result from innate qualities which favor men over women, Roder and the Munroes may indeed be justified in suggesting that the low numbers of women in the spatial professions is not surprising. What woman, knowing she has an inherent disadvantage because of her genetic make-up, would choose a profession where failure is such a high probability? Perhaps we should advise women to stay away from such professions entirely.

Few would agree with such an extreme position, just as few would advise men to avoid professions where language skills lead to success because girls develop language earlier than boys (which statistics show is the case). Harris (1979:171) investigated, with exhaustive thoroughness, numerous possible reasons why sex differences in spatial abilities exist, and concluded "there is no single, simple explanation for sex differences in spatial ability." Harris and others find evidence for a biological base to these differences, but emphasize that much also points to conditioning, which would weaken the argument for innateness of differences. In any event, the innate deficiencies of spatial abilities which women might possess can be reduced or eliminated through education and training programs designed to develop spatial skills (Wrightman and Deaux 1981:412).

We do not know whether low scores on spatial tests are innate; we do know, however, that spatial ability differences are only valid for average individuals of large populations. As with the results of most psychological tests, there is a wide variation above and below the means for both sexes. So even if we were to agree that, on the average, boys are better at spatial problems than girls, we must recognize that a vast number of women score *higher* than an equally vast number of men. One has the nagging fear that many young women, who are considering a spatial profession, may be dissuaded by counselors who generalize from the characteristics of women *as a whole* when advising *individuals*. Armed with notions of inherent average female inferiority, advisors are likely to suggest the ambitions of talented females are unrealistic. Furthermore, no studies have been made which link success in the spatial professions with test scores on spatial ability measures. So we do not know if the heightened spatial ability of the average boy is of much value at the advanced level.

We do know, however, that until recently women were denied the opportunity to enter these professions. Entrance into professional schools was difficult, and women generally were not given the encouragement to strive for success in these areas. In Chapter 4 we show that few women have become architects and urban planners, and we demonstrate that the buildings and urban form of America disadvantage women. Women interested in design have been directed to take up professions with lower status and pay than architecture and planning; this is the "social discrimination" to which Roder refers.

Specialists themselves admit that the research on spatial abilities is inconclusive and generates many more questions than answers. We might conclude, then, it would be best to wait until the biologists and psychologists have done more research before we attempt to make sense of the scant data now available. While the behavioral scientists continue trying to discover which sex differences are innate and which are caused by inequality in social conditioning, the rest of us might better use our energies to eliminate the "social discrimination" we see around us. We may very well find, when given early encouragement and full access to education, women will be as able as men to achieve success in the spatial professions such as architecture, engineering, urban and landscape design — and *geography*.

4

Her Role in Changing the Face of the Earth

When we look at a landscape we observe the landforms, lakes, wild vegetation, and other elements of the natural environment. We also observe (unless it is remote wilderness indeed) the effects of human occupancy: roads, bridges, fences, dwellings, and other structures which reveal human presence. The landscape of human creation we call the cultural landscape, as opposed to the natural landscape. Geographers have long been concerned with the modification of the natural landscape by human activity. In 1956, a major publication appeared, *Man's Role in Changing the Face of the Earth* (Thomas 1956). The term "man" undoubtedly was intended in its generic sense, as a synonym of "human." Unfortunately, however, not all read "man" in this sense, and concluded that the human modification of the earth resulted only from male pursuits and activities. Recently geographers have wondered how gender does affect landscape. In this chapter this matter is discussed, and attention is directed to the role of women in changing the natural landscape and in creating the features of the cultural landscape.

Landscape and Food Production

Most of human history has been spent in the stage of development called the paleolithic ("old stone age") which began when humankind evolved distinct from other ape-like creatures and made crude stone tools. Generally it ended with the invention of agriculture, although in some remote locales the paleolithic survives today. During that long period, some of our most basic advancements took place: language, fire, tools, and shelter to name a few.

What was early human society like? No one knows for sure, of course, but two images by prominent geographers are presented here. Broek and Webb (1978:48) suggest:

The division of labor between the sexes and the sharing of food became a feature of human existence. The women, however, foraged around their campsites for roots, seeds, berries, and edible leaves as well as for grubs and easily caught creatures. The men were the hunters, roaming over much wider areas, banding together to overpower the prey, and sharing the kill among themselves and their families.

Carter (1975:37-8) also commented on paleolithic division of labor. Hunting, he says, was "a man's game." It suited man's personality. It was a gambler's game because the reward of stalking and waiting for the prey is unassured: "there is a half-ton of meat in a pot — or nothing." As for women, he says, "the gathering of roots and seeds and berries was the woman's work. . . . She may not make a killing at seed gathering, but there will surely be a little gruel for everyone." The nature of our paleolithic origins can only be inferred by studying contemporary paleolithic groups, and by reading the archeological record. The pictures presented above, however, give us a biased image, drudgery for women and excitement for men, as if paleolithic society naturally had the same discriminatory division of labor as contemporary society. Carter talks of the labor of men as a "game," whereas females were engaged in "women's work." Given the choice between the challenge and stimulation of the hunt or the making of gruel and grubbing for insects, few today of either sex would choose the latter, and few would award equal status to both activities. Hunting suggests travel to exotic landscapes; today it is a stimulating form of recreation held in high esteem by millions and primarily oriented toward the male sex. Grubbing and gruel making would be noxious pursuits, devoid of any romance or excitement.

Moreover, this picture overemphasizes the importance of hunting to the diet of paleolithic society. The anthropologist Elizabeth Fisher (1979:57,72) discovered that one account of a contemporary Australian group devoted five times the space to describing the hunt than to food gathering, though the latter provided about *70 percent* of the food. Except in the arctic, gathering is far more important than hunting among paleolithic peoples. Yet the importance of gathering has been overlooked in descriptions which romanticize man's labor and reinforce contemporary stereotypes of women as stone-age housewives (Tanner 1981; Chapter 9; Zihlman 1978).

During the paleolithic, changes to human society came slowly. Inventions and discoveries allowed humans to use the environment more effectively than their ancestors. The discovery of the importance of fire probably resulted after a natural conflagration swept an area. Cautiously humans began poking in the ashes. Food products caught in the accidental fire would smell good, so women (assuming they were the food preparers) would recognize the value of fire for cooking. Other uses of fire evolved later (Fisher 1979:66-7). The origin of tools is also open to speculation, and the story presented in many texts reflect a male bias. The crude pieces of flint associated with paleolithic humans have been thought to be hunting tools. Tanner and Zihlman (quoted in Eby 1979:23) examine this issue:

> *Anthropologists have simply assumed that prehistoric tools were designed by men to wage battle with animals. However, no one has ever been able to explain exactly how these implements might have been put to that purpose (see also Tanner and Zihlman 1976:599-602; Fisher 1979:63-4).*

Stone tools, they contend, were invented to help in gathering, not the hunting of food, and thus apparently can be credited to women.

Stone tools are a small part of paleolithic human's "kit." Much of what constituted tools were made of perishable materials such as plant material, leather, and hair. The earliest tool may have been some sort of container, first probably out of a large leaf, a piece of bark, or some other natural substance (advanced, non-human primates use such containers today). Later containers would have been fashioned with more sophistication. One early use of the container would have been as a sling to carry a baby so as to free a mother's hands for gathering and other work. Game animals could be dragged to camp, so containers logically would not have been invented by man-the-hunter (Fisher 1979:60; Tanner and Zihlman 1976:600; Tanner 1981: Chapter 9).

Paleolithic modification of the natural landscape would have been minimal, at least compared with the effects of later inventions. However, a revised picture of paleolithic society suggests that those landscape alterations which did occur could have resulted from female pursuits. Long before agriculture and plant domestication, for example, natural vegetation would have been altered by selective gathering of plants by women. Tanner (1981:222) says that:

> *Because of nutritional requirements of pregnancy and nursing and overt demands from hungry children, women had more motivation for technological inventiveness, for creativity in dealing with the environment, for learning about plants, and for developing tools to increase productivity and save time.*

Tanner's words are reminiscent of those of Carl Sauer (1963:308) nearly twenty years earlier:

> *As long as the mother bore children, and also beyond such time, she had the feeding and care of the young to look after. In her daily foraging she carried or was accompanied by her brood, the older ones learning from her what was good and how to secure it. She discovered the first hard rule of economic geography, the cost of distance. Hers was the greater necessity to learn the use of tools, digging stick, handstone, and club.*

Major modifications of landscape occurred with the development of agriculture, which took place about ten thousand years ago during the neolithic. Crop cultivation evolved slowly and grew out of the gathering tradition. Therefore, farming very probably was originally a female occupation. Early farming was a type of horticulture, which involved digging sticks, hoes, and other simple hand tools. Clearing the land of its wild vegetation would have been done by the men of the society (so we assume generalizing from contemporary horticultural groups), but once the land was cleared, the women would have participated in the planting and harvesting. Today, in virtually all horticultural societies the women (or women and men together) do the planting and harvesting (Friedl 1975:53-8). Women would have been involved in the decisions which affected the form of the landscape, choosing the crops, and designing the layout of the fields, which were small and conformed to the smooth contours of the land. Later came the invention of the plow. Plow agriculture was man's activity. He chose the crops. The fields he plowed were straight-lined, regularized, geometrical. Plow agriculture diffused from its Middle East hearth throughout the middle latitudes, where most of the world's food is grown, and as it expanded, the importance of women in agriculture decreased.

Through the millennia thousands of refinements changed agriculture to what it is today. Modern farming is highly mechanized. Crop plants are hybrids requiring chemical fertilizers. The choice of what crop to grow is based in part on economic projections made far from the site of production. All the professions which impact on modern farming — such as agronomy, farm-machinery engineering, agricultural economics, and commodity trading — have been the near-exclusive domains of men. Moreover, farms themselves are owned primarily by men. Farmers and farm managers in the United States are men, ten to one (U.S. Census 1980: Table 8-1). The farming landscape, which thousands of years ago reflected the accomplishments of women, is today, in modern societies, the creation of men.

In the developing world, however, women still contribute greatly to food production. It is estimated, for example, that 70 percent of the agricultural labor force of Africa is women (Women's Programme Unit 1975:4). The proportion is smaller in Latin America (40 percent) but still significant (Tinker 1981:53,69). Under traditional patterns, women farmers retain much control over crop selection and other land use decisions and, thus, are similar to the early horticulturists in this regard. Traditional patterns are breaking down, though, as modernization invades the rural scene in the third world.

Modernization has many effects, some of which benefit women and men alike, many of which benefit men to the exclusion of women. Both men and women are unfamiliar with machines in many rural, Third World areas. However, women are thought incapable of running machinery, so they do not receive the same training in mechanization as do men. Therefore, the rewards which may result from mechanized farming are not as likely to accrue to the women as to the men. Further, mechanization allows farmers to cultivate larger acreages. This means forests are pushed back (probably necessitating a longer walk for the women for firewood). New fields resulting from mechanization take on a 'modern' look, unlike the traditional plots which women help design.

Another impact of modernization in Third World agriculture is the expansion of cash crops, such as rubber, bananas, pineapples, and many others. Cash crop cultivation is often controlled by men, whereas subsistence cultivation is women's work. In Kenya, for example, 95 percent of the food is produced by women (Tinker 1981:56). Strobel (1982:112) says:

> Although women sometimes sold and bartered surplus foods, the growth of such cash crops as cotton, cocoa, and coffee came to be dominated and controlled by men. Colonial agricultural officers, with their sexist assumptions about the division of labor, gave information and seed to men.

Government agents would spread enthusiasm among male farmers to grow cash crops, causing the amount of land devoted to cash crops to increase at the expense of subsistence crop land. So women would have to work harder to grow the family's food needs. The money which men realize from the cash crops may benefit the entire family, but problems arise when men "use this money for improving homes, throwing 'prestige' feasts, (or) buying transistor radios" (Tinker 1981:63). Unfortunately, men also squander the wealth on "gambling, liquor, and women." Moreover, modernization bypasses women because women work extremely long hours and have little free time for such diversions as learning about cash crops and modern agriculture. Men work six to sixteen fewer hours per day than women on the average (International Labor Organization 1981:39).

In the developing world we see the position of rural women undergoing change, not always for the better. With modernization, decisions which affect the landscape are becoming more and more removed from local authority where the impact of women is great (Mead 1976:9-10). The importance of women as food producers is too frequently deemed insignificant, and women's labor is considered backward. This opinion is expressed not only by Third World males, but by western academics as well. The French geographer, Aime Perpillou, took a dim view of African farming systems: "Such a division of labor which leaves the burden of cultivation on women condemns native agriculture in Central and East Africa to a state of irretrievable weakness." Since cultivation activity "lacks man's strength and is left to the weak hands of women," he says, "it loses the advantage of more efficient work" (Perpillou 1977:150). The idea of "development," then, reflects both western and local native biases against women and too often means replacing the contributions of women with modern, but perhaps less efficient, masculine pursuits. This leads to a decline in food production, the very effect which the food technology planners wish to reverse. Irene Tinker (1981:57) says, "In order for the food crisis strategies to accomplish their goal of feeding the world, women must not only be included in planning, they must be central to it."

Women and the Built Environment

The built environment is that part of the total environment which has been modified by human construction. Such construction may involve impressive, immense structures such as dams and skyscrapers. It may be humble village houses. Or it may be very subtle alterations of the natural landscape such as a bare plot of land which serves as a village soccer field. In any event, built environments testify to human presence, and result from human desire to design and build.

House Form

Prominent on the cultural landscape are human habitations. The earliest human shelters may have been simple rock shelters, which Carl Sauer (1963:308-9) suggested were originally constructed by mothers to shelter their young. Possibly shelters were simple nests, like ones which non-human primates construct for their young. Fisher (1979:64-5) stated:

> The temporary windbreak or shelter made from branches was another invention that would grow almost naturally out of the primate's nest-making ability. Even today it is women who are responsible for building windbreaks or branch huts among such foraging groups as the Mbuti Pygmies and the Kalahari San, as well as among many groups, both foraging and horticultural, with much more advanced techniques.

North American Indian women were often the architects of their communities, especially in the plains and southwest. The tipi, for example, the distinctive dwelling of plains cultures, was the creation of women. "A tipi was not only beautiful but practical, being one of the most efficient shelters for a migrant people," (Cole 1973:5). It is sturdy, well ventilated, easily erected from local environmental elements, and easily taken down and transported. In the southwest, the elaborate stone and mud structures of Pueblo cultures were also the product of women: "The Pueblo woman builds her house of stone or adobe. Her agile hands are the whole kit of mason's tools for fitting the materials and smoothing the walls" (Joyce 1908:445).

But worldwide the builders of houses usually are men. Perhaps as with tools and agriculture, the innovation which began with women was taken over by men. In the Nile Valley of Egypt and northern Sudan, where building materials and overall house form are similar to the Pueblo's, the builders are male. The house in the Nile Valley consists of flat-roofed, mud-walled, rectangular rooms surrounded by a five-foot high wall (Figure 16). Many theories attempt to explain the origin of the courtyard house along the Nile, but it seems clear that it is related to notions of privacy and the male insistence upon female seclusion. Along this reach of the Nile, from central Sudan to the Delta, the

FIGURE 16   TYPICAL HOUSEHOLD LAYOUT, THE NILE VALLEY IN NORTHERN SUDAN (from field notes of D. R. Lee).

people are Muslim Arabs. In Muslim society great emphasis is placed on female purity. Pre- and extra-marital sexual intercourse is fanatically condemned, and considered such a disgrace that an indiscreet female would be reprimanded if caught merely displaying body language which we might call innocuous flirtation. A female guilty of illicit sexual behavior would surely be beaten, perhaps even murdered by her family for her indiscretion. From this extreme attitude came the seclusion institution: males feel it is their duty to keep the women secluded as much as possible from all contact with men who are not immediate members of the family. The rationale is that if the women are kept out of sight they cannot be compromised. When women are in the streets, therefore, they walk briskly to their destination, with no dallying en route. Traditional Muslim women wear long robes which cover the body except for hands and eyes — the veil institution of Muslim society (of which more is said below).

Outdoors the women are heavily clothed, but at home, the women dress more casually, as the geographer Ellsworth Huntington discovered in Khartoum: "A glimpse through a door inadvertently left open may disclose a woman stripped to the waist in order to work comfortably. That same woman would be heavily veiled on the street" (Huntington 1959:303). The courtyard wall of the Sudanese house, therefore, functions as a device to insure female privacy — and purity (Lee 1967:261).

Within courtyard walls, the household is further subdivided into those where men frequent, and those where the women attend to their affairs. The man's court is used to entertain other men, and when a stranger is in the court the women may not intrude. The entrance to the man's court is a gate, above which rests an elaborate molded mud decoration, often carrying plates or other decorative items. In order that the women may exit the household without passing through the men's court, a smaller door, lacking the molded decoration, is provided in the outside wall of the women's court.

Polygyny, another institution practiced both among Muslims and non-Muslims in Africa, also impacts on the domestic landscape. Among the Tallensi of northern Ghana, a man may have two or more wives. Each wife has her own round room as well as her own kitchens, one for the wet season, and one for the dry season (Figure 17). Should the patriarch take an additional wife, the walls would be knocked down on one side and the compound would be expanded so the new wife could have her room and kitchens as well (Prussin 1972:58-9). Polygyny in the Near East recalls the Arab and Turkish harem. The term 'harem' suggests the wives, concubines, and female servants kept by a man of means, but it also refers to the quarters where these women dwell. In the humble mud dwellings of West Africa or the Nile Valley, the harem is simply the women's courtyard. In more elaborate town houses, the harem may consist of large,

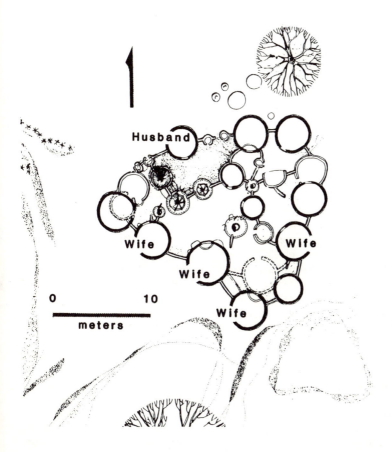

FIGURE 17   A TALLENSI COMPOUND, NORTHERN GHANA (from Prussin 1972: Figure 3-6; reproduced by permission of the University of California Press).

secluded quarters which overlook the central man's court. In order that the women may observe the goings-on below, intricately carved wooden shutters are placed over the harem windows; the women may look and listen through small holes in the shutters but strangers in the court are unable to observe the women. Here again, the form of the Muslim house reflects the demands for female seclusion.

Architecture reflects polygyny (or lack of it) elsewhere in the world as well. In Cameroon, for example, the home of a polygynous household is distinct from that of a monogynous one (Figure 18, Beguin and Kalt 1952:19, 52). In polygynous households, each wife usually has her own separate room; the husband sleeps with a different wife on some sort of a rotation basis. In fact, he may have no real room of his own.

Polygyny was practiced in the United States by Mormons, and folklore had it that the Mormon house reflected the institution. Brigham Young's house in Salt Lake City was said to have had a separate dormer window for each of his many wives. In Morman villages, the older brick houses commonly had two front doors, supposedly one for each of two wives. These architectural details, however, are actually unrelated to early Mormon polygyny.

Many of the architectural forms examined thus far would seem to demonstrate impacts of women on landscape which result from calculated and conscious design decisions. Sometimes unconscious processes affect the landscape. For example, in West Africa the form of earthen granaries takes on Freudian meaning. The bins for grain storage commonly are huge earthen structures, larger than pots but smaller than rooms. Some clearly suggest femininity; the shape may recall a pregnant woman: full and rounded, tight skinned, ready to burst forth with life. Surface decoration in mud or paint may be explicit. Among the Lobi, for example, "female attributes, breats, vulva, face, representing the essence of womanhood, clearly express the metaphysical assocation between the granary form, its contents, and femininity" (Prussin 1969:159). Among other groups, male references are found. For the Tayaba, for example, the seed of the granary has suggested semen, and the granary form is phallic (Figure 19). Freudian psychology has revealed the unconscious human tendency to design artifacts to suggest the phallus, and phallic symbols are common. Indeed, to novice Freudians they may seem to appear everywhere. Archaeologists often dub virtually all long round object as "penis objects" (Fisher 1979:249), and architectural historians do likewise. This tendency to see phalluses in all constructions which have a pronounced vertical element (such as minarets, skyscrapers, telephone poles and the like) may strike some as undue and unjustified concern to find symbolism where none exists. Freud himself is reported to have said, "gentlemen, sometimes a cigar is just a cigar" (Fisher 1979: 24). However, with respect to the Tayaba granary, the symbolic connection is unmistakable. Their granaries clearly are male sex organs writ large.

Clothing patterns give character and variety to landscapes, and attitudes toward women, architecture, and clothing patterns are often interrelated. How people dress is in large part related to their concepts of modesty, and what is considered acceptable in one society may be scandalous in another. Muslims insist that women must be veiled and remain segregated to isolated quarters, but African women (at least before European arrival) often went bare-breasted and generally enjoyed a freedom of movement outside the home which was denied to Arabs. European and American customs permit women to expose a discrete amount of the body. The total face, the arms, and the lower legs can be exposed, even with formal dress. Informal dress, especially beach wear, may expose perhaps 95 percent of the female body. But beyond that one may not go. Laws virtually everywhere require the nipples and genital

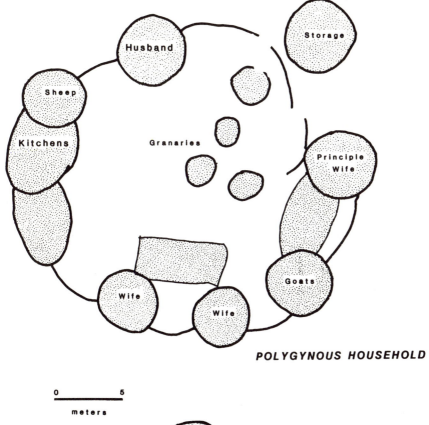

POLYGYNOUS HOUSEHOLD

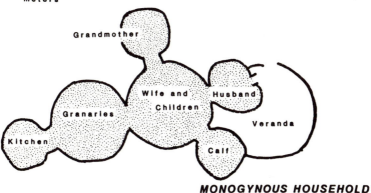

MONOGYNOUS HOUSEHOLD

FIGURE 18   POLYGYNOUS AND MONOGYNOUS
HOUSEHOLDS IN CAMEROON. Shaded areas are roofed
(after drawings in Beguin *et al.* 1952: 19, 52).

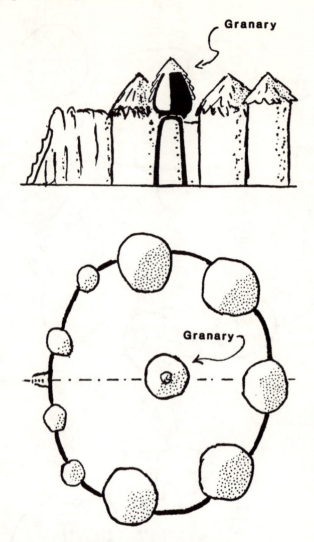

FIGURE 19   TAYABA COMPOUND AND GRANARY, NORTHERN BENIN (DAHOMEY). The section (top drawing) is taken along the broken line shown in the plan of the compound (bottom drawing) (after Mercier 1954: Figure XII).

area be kept from view. Today's informal attire would have shocked nineteenth century Europeans and does shock contemporary Arabs. Westerners may scoff at Arab prudishness, but western women themselves would be ill at ease with African barebreastedness. Yet Africans would find traditional Japanese customs extreme. Amos Rapoport (1969:66) stated:

Traditional Japan, before western influence, had a very different idea of modesty, and hence of privacy. During the summer people would appear naked in public, and used common baths; during the same season one could look right through farmhouses.

Rapoport emphasized that few elements in house form are universal to all societies. We tend to think that one of the most basic functions of the dwelling is privacy, yet clearly modesty and privacy notions vary greatly. So, too, do house elements related to these notions.

Women in Africa, especially compared with Arab women, enjoy high status. They engage in trade and become entrepreneurs. They take responsibility for food production, as examined earlier. Among approximately one-third of African societies, the women build the houses (Women's Programme Unit 1975:6). Whereas in Arab society the image of women — the symbol of female — is one of impurity and shame, in Africa the female image is wholesome and positive. Outside African houses, yard shrines carved in wood embellish the domestic landscape. Commonly these take the form of a female figure, often with exaggerated breasts to honor motherhood and the role of the female in reproduction. To Arabs and to Christian missionaries, such sculptures appeared to be disgustingly pornographic. When either group attained control in an African locality, the female yard shrines disappeared.

Yard shrines also adorn house yards in Latin countries. These are the statues representing Catholic saints, the Madonna, and Jesus. Sometimes the shrines are tiny, sometimes elaborate. Though sacred personages of both sexes are represented, most commonly the shrines honor female figures. In the Cuban district of Miami, for example, by far the most common are Santa Barbara and Our Lady of Charity, patron saint of Cuba (Curtis 1980:5). The Latin residential district of Miami can be identified from the street by the presence of these statues, which testify to the adoration which Cubans have for these female figures.

Proper female conduct is of concern in all societies. Rules are set down to regulate all types of behavior, even how a woman may properly menstruate. Many peoples believe that menstruation is an unclean act, and the menstruating woman herself is contaminated. Therefore, she is provided with a disconnected room of the household known as the women's lodge, or hut, where she goes during the menstrual period. Among North American Indians, the Athabascans believed:

The woman or girl was dangerous both to herself and the world at that this time. . . . The girl could not look out upon the world during her condition lest she blight it and drive game away. . . . Hence she not only remained in the seclusion hut but often wore a hood or a veil, being careful to keep her eyes cast down (Spencer and Jennings 1977:110).

Many North American Indians had such structures. They would be built some distance from other structures and would face away from them. Some groups provided large lodges for many women which served as menstruation rooms and were birthing places as well. Isolation of menstruating women was found elsewhere as well. Among high caste Hindus, for example, a special room within the household was reserved for this purpose (Hirt 1978). In the West the repugnance of menstruation has not manifested itself with architectural expressions such as these. Americans today are open about the subject; indeed, television commercials for tampons and sanitary napkins shout the virtues of their products with extreme frankness. This would have shocked polite society a few years ago when talk on the subject was taboo.

The American landscape owes much of its unique character to the form of its habitations. The American house has a rich history, from simple colonial antecedents, to the ornate Victorian dwelling, to eclecticism of recent styles. For each period, and for each style, architectural historians have traced the origin and meaning of particular elements of house form. Religious asceticism accounts for New England simplicity, whereas love of European elegance produced southern mansions. Regional influences are common. The bungalow of the 1920s has its origins in houses which the British found in India, whereas stucco homes of the 1930s are distant cousins to Spanish prototypes. Virtually none of the house forms, however, or even specific design elements can be connected to women. The few items mentioned below are included to illustrate the paucity, not the richness, of female-related influences.

One feature found on some New England colonial houses and later copies of these was the "widow's walk," a platform or walkway enclosed by a railing, constructed over the peaked roof of a house (Harrison 1973:411). Supposedly this balcony-like platform allowed the wife of a sea captain to view the ocean from many directions. She would search the seas for her husband's returning ship. If his vessel were lost, the widow might walk the platform forever, waiting for a ship which would never come.

One searches in vain to find other examples of house forms which reflect women. Throughout our history, house design and house construction have been the special sphere of men. In the early nineteenth century America had few trained architects, and builders relied on handbooks designed to help the novice, which at first were written by men exclusively. As the century progressed, more and more handbooks and magazines on architecture were written by women, for women. However, the books and magazines were mainly concerned with interiors (Cole 1973:23,33-4; Rock *et al.* 1980).

In post-civil War times, the role of women in architecture improved only slightly. Blanchard Bethuen became the first woman member of the American Institute of Architects in 1888. Earlier, Catherine Beecher's work on the American woman's home (1869) included numerous plans and renderings of facades. Her 'gothic' dwelling is well designed and in keeping with the styles of the times. It had a church-like appearance and emphasized the self-sacrificing role of women as wives and mothers, which Beecher supported (Hayden 1977:44-5; *Ms. Magazine* 1977).

Some construction of the 19th century reveals revolutionary attitudes toward women. The dwellings of communes and socialist utopian communities, of which there were hundreds, are examples (Cole 1973:61). The organization and *raison d'etre* of each was unique, but common to most was the principle of equality for all, irrespective of age, race, and sex. They were unique sociologically as well as architecturally:

> *In contrast to the private houses which these domestic reformers denounced as isolated, wasteful, and oppressive, they hoped to build communal or cooperative facilities for domestic work — tangible, architectural demonstrations of the workings of a more egalitarian society (Hayden 1980a:104).*

In the Oneida Community of New York, women had a great deal of freedom compared with their contemporaries outside (Cole 1973:64). To free the wife from domestic drudgery, food was cooked in large central kitchen and eaten in a large communal dining hall. (Hayden 1980a:106). The Amana community in Iowa also employed communal kitchens for eight or ten women. A most intriguing design was that of the Llano del Rio community of California, whose plan called for a radial street pattern with a huge kitchen at the hub. Hot food would be shipped via an underground railroad to kitchenless houses. Again, the objective of the design was to free the wife from cooking (Hayden 1978:283-7).

These experiments in feminist design are important because they show that there was concern with the role of women and the layout of domestic space. They had no lasting effect, however, in altering the form of the cultural landscape.

The 19th century saw a tremendous growth in the American city. Especially toward the end of the century, the urban house presented women with many amenities. For the rich with servants, the beautiful Victorian mansions provided comfortable elegance. For the less well off, smaller single-family dwellings were available, although they were expensive. Single women, who arrived from the farms, lived in boarding houses or lodging houses. The latter provided young women a great measure of freedom; they could live alone and take meals in restaurants in the neighborhood (Rothman 1978:90-91). For middle-class families, the apartment house became available late in the nineteenth century. This structure made life easier for the wife. They were easier to maintain than single-family houses and contained modern advancements such as hot water, toilets, and kitchen appliances. The increased density of the city required elaborate innovations in marketing as well. The department store began to replace the small, single-function shop. Designed to appeal to the female consumer, the department store made a day of shopping, with lunch downtown, a pleasurable break from day-to-day routine (Rothman 1978:14-15,18).

Suburban developments were also available to those who wished to leave the cities. From mid-19th century on, suburbs were built on rail lines which provided convenient service into towns, allowing men to work in the city and have their families living in the country. Suburban living was appealing for its isolation, openness, and fresh air (Cole 1973:41).

In the twentieth century the popularity of the suburbs increased. Commuting was facilitated by the private automobile, and large areas of cheap land away from railroad lines were devoted to low density housing. The "American dream" more and more became a bungalow in the suburbs. While the husband was at work, the wife was supposed to create a pleasant domestic environment. Returning from his exhausting day at the office, he could collapse and be waited upon by his dutiful wife. World War II disrupted this pattern as women worked in wartime industries, but following the war came the return of the GI's and tremendous suburban expansion.

Cities and suburbs presented contrasting images which reflected the people they supposedly attracted. The cities were considered to be masculine: active, powerful, assertive. Important matters were decided here. The suburbs, on the other hand, were feminine: safe but frivolous, mindless, passive. In the suburbs one was insulated from the conflicts of the outside world (Saegert 1980:96). The suburban house reflected and reinforced this isolation and withdrawal from public life by its very form and location. It was detached from other dwellings, centered in the large house lot. The secluded backyard patio became the focus of family activity, replacing the open front porch of earlier homes (Rothman 1978:225). Houses were dispersed, making shopping locations and houses of friends difficult to reach. In earlier times, one could walk to a market or a friend's home, but in the sprawling suburbs this was no longer possible. Moreover, public transportation was lacking or grossly inadequate, and in one-car families, the mobility of the wife was limited. Even with a car, she was restricted because shopping and car pooling consumed much of her day. Suburban housewives have been called the "new servant class," spending endless hours chauffeuring children to lessons, appointments, and friends' homes. To many women, intellectual stagnation became a problem. Whereas the urban woman could easily obtain stimulation in the museums and theaters of the city, the suburban woman could only attend such events with difficulty. Daytime TV offered pallid substitutes.

Further, employment outside the house was most difficult. For many suburban women, restricted horizontal mobility meant restricted opportunity and restricted upward mobility. Industries located in the central cities were hard for a suburban housewife to reach. If she had children, the continual question was what to do with the kids while mommy was at work. Women who may have invested years of education toward a career suddenly found that positions were difficult to find. They accepted lower-paying jobs near home, took part-time positions, or simply did not work at all. This applied to professionals — lawyers, physicians, accountants, even geographers (Epstein, 1970:136). Blue collar women were affected as well. In one study, a third of the blue collar women studied worked when the family lived in the city, but after the move to the suburbs, only 18 percent took jobs (Fava 1980:136).

As the suburbs expanded farther and farther from the central city, the time required for the husband's commute increased; and, concomitantly, his input to household maintenance became smaller and smaller. Among families that had moved from the central city to the suburbs, the husbands were far more satisfied with their new homes than were the wives (Fava 1980:135; Loyd 1982). Men liked the relaxed atmosphere and outdoor living. The women disliked the prospects of isolation from urban amenities, intellectual stagnation, and boredom. Likewise, Tognoli (1979:603) reported that:

> In studies of the responses of suburban and urban residents to their environments, (researchers) found that men were more satisfied with suburban locations than women. The women reported feeling both an intellectual and a social isolation in the suburbs and often expressed fears before the move from the city that they were not looking forward to it and that they were bound to encounter isolation and boredom. The move was primarily done for the husband's sake, who expressed optimism about the move and expected a more relaxed environment and a better place for his children to grow up in.

The single-family suburban house types, with practically no exceptions, were designed by men. Women interested in design professions traditionally were encouraged to concern themselves with interiors and leave the complicated details of overall construction and exterior design to men (Arnett 1975). A few women did achieve success in architecture, to be sure. Sophia Hayden created the expansive and aesthetically successful Woman's Building at the 1893 world exposition in Chicago. Julia Morgan designed the remarkable San Simeon "castle" owned by William Randolph Hearst, which today is one of the most popular tourist attractions on the California coast between San Francisco and Los Angeles (Paine 1977:57; Boutelle 1977:80-83). But for the most part, architects were men. The appearance of the structures in the residential landscape resulted from the designs conceived by males.

However, one aspect of the suburban landscape is the responsibility of women: the garden. A garden becomes the woman's "personal landscape," a medium for her creative idiosyncracies and aesthetic sensitivities (Jacobs 1980:16; Pochoda, 1979). Women select the appropriate plantings to surround the house. Women design the overall layout. Women care for the garden and nurture the plants through the seasons.

Monthlies like *Better Homes and Gardens* and *House and Garden* clearly are directed toward a female audience. The suburban landscape, then, is an intriguing mixture of inputs from male house designers and women gardeners.

How is it that the sprawling suburbs came to dominate the American landscape? There are many explanations, but an intriguing case has been made that the pattern was purposely designed to met the perceived needs of a family which had the woman trapped at home with the kids. The suburban structure benefits men by providing an opportunity for them to partake of urban amenities and avoid domestic responsibilities. At the same time it limits women's freedom, making them accept the happy-wife-at-home model of women because they lack options. Suburban design was and still is discriminatory. This sentiment is expressed in the following

> . . . *Seen from the perspective of a woman struggling to assert her-self . . ., it seems very much as if men prefer to go on creating and maintaining environments that inhibit women's attempts to broaden their roles and activities (Wekerle et al. 1980:13).*

> . . . *The private suburban house was the stage set for the effective sexual division of labor . . . capitalism and antifeminism fused in campaigns for home ownership and mass consumption: the patriarch whose home was his "castle" was to work year in and year out to provide the wages to support this private environment (Hayden 1980b:172).*

This argument (that suburbs were purposely designed to subjugate women) is an extreme position. Irene Bruegel criticizes Pat Burnett (1973) for suggesting that urban form can only be explained by man's "lust for power which explains women's sub-jugated position in society and hence their subordination in the structuring of the city. . . ." (Bruegel 1973:73):

> *By concentrating on male dominance as the major factor explaining women's position in the urban structure, Pat [Burnett] would seem to imply that if women took the decisions, this would in itself alter the structure of the city. But given the dynamic of the capitalist system, it is unclear why women wouldn't be constrained to creating a profit-maximizing city structure (Bruegel, 1973, p. 63).*

Where the truth might lie is difficult to assess. Would a city designed by women be significantly different than the male designed ones standing now? Bowlby and colleagues reported that some women ". . . see liberation only in a society of complete gender separation and this has led to demands for concomitant changes in the built environment" (Bowlby *et al.* 1981:20). Theories may abound, but few facts present themselves. Notwithstanding, the theories introduce some intriguing topics and merit examination.

Many contend that the suburban landscape of the future could be designed to better accommodate the needs of women. The present American pattern is by no means universal or inevitable. European housing has long emphasized apartment complexes and high density single-family units, as in Sweden, for example. The overall population density is far greater than in American suburbs. Because the suburbs are compact, women can walk or bike to retail and service centers. Day care facilities are easily reached. Moreover, the suburbs are linked by outstanding transportation to central cities. Thus, women can conveniently take advantage of the cultural attractions in town (Popenoe 1980:166,169; Werner 1980:176,186; Epstein 1970:133).

Elsewhere — in England, Canada, and the United States, for example — projects have been proposed (and a few built) with the needs of women in mind. They are innovative and provide for child care facilities, but they are also costly. Existing suburban blocks could be modified at very little cost, however, better to meet the needs of women with children, single women, and the elderly. One design calls for reducing the number of automobiles (and their driveways and garages) and adding two "dial-a-ride" vans, thus providing transportation to those without cars. Backyard fences would be torn down so that space could be used collectively, especially by children. Certain services, such as a day care facility and a food cooperative, would be established (Figure 20; Hayden 1980b:S181-S187). Potential designs may appear radical, but whether or not one pictures onself accepting such a totally altered environment, one must be intrigued by the potential advantages it offers, particularly for women.

The chances that women can significantly alter the landscape are slim, at least given the design professions as they now stand. Women constitute but two percent of practicing architects (Loyd 1982:193). Among these, many are relegated to designing interiors. Loyd (1982:193) says that the reason for this lies in the history of the profession:

> In recent decades the struggle to professionalize architecture led to an emphasis on monumental structures and sculptural design as well as a buildings and office towers receive honors and large commissions. Housing stays on the back burner. Male architects produce buildings that enlarge their reputations and sculpt the exterior public landscape. Interiors, the domain of women and their families, receive scant attention.

Urban planners also are overwhelmingly male, as are civic leaders who can influence decisions on building codes and zoning regulations. Morley (1980:204) expresses concern about this situation and indicates that it is difficult to reflect on women in planning and architecture "without a feeling of gloom and despondence." Institutions which create or modify environments, he says, are "the tools of the existing male-dominated society. They create environments that are symbols of that societal authority."

It is ironic that in many regards, the detached, isolated, single-family house is more discriminatory against American females than is the Arab house against Arab women. In the latter, the prevalence of large extended families living together, and the institution of the harem, provide for fellowship and sharing of tasks among the many women of the family. The term "harem" may suggest a system of sexual access for males, but it is also a system whereby women have living space *beyond* the domination of men (Ahmed 1982:524). Group work and specialization of labor in the household mean housework may be more enjoyable and efficient than the American pattern, where one wife does everything. In the Arab house, child care is not burdensome because plenty of baby-sitters are available. The generally high dwelling density of Arab towns and villages facilitates travel by foot, so the women can reach the shops and houses of friends easily. Housework, especially in village houses, is treated more casually than in the American household. For example, many traditional houses and courtyards have dirt floors, and dirt and dust are an accepted part of living. There is consequently no preoccupation with superfluous spotlessness, as there is in the West. This is not to say, of course, that the households in developing nations are superior to those in America. Indeed not, living standards are low. Much time must be spent drawing water, gathering

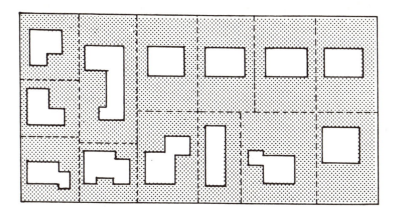

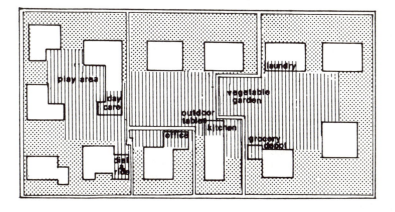

private space :::::

collective space |||||

FIGURE 20 REVITALIZATION PROJECT OF HOMES (Homemakers Organization for a More Egalitarian Society). The existing suburban neighborhood block plan (top drawing) would be redesigned with new common space and facilities (bottom drawing) (from Hayden 1980b: Figure 5; used by permission of *Signs* and The University of Chicago Press).

wood, and engaging in other menial tasks. Although dirt floors may be easy to care for, they are unsanitary. Work is hard and living conditions are wretched, but probably no worse than for others at the same economic level, say, for example, for women from an isolated subsistence farm in Appalachia. Nevertheless, although life is harsh in Arab households, there are social advantages not found in the West.

Other Landscape Structures

Discussion thus far on the impact of women on the form of the built environment has centered on the house and residential location. Women (and men's attitudes toward women) are reflected in artifacts beyond the home as well. Certain structures are known to be associated with men, others are for women. They carry visual clues which communicate the gender distinction. These features give visual proof that women and men live in different worlds.

The landscape of India contains one such gender-specific artifact. In some areas, *sati* shrines seem ubiquitous. The shrines, usually about the size of a tombstone but often larger, reveal that a woman has committed *sati;* that is, upon the death of her husband, she threw herself upon the man's funeral fire, thus burning herself to death. Though *sati* is now outlawed, the shrines are grim reminders of an institution which asserted that a woman would be blessed if she would commit suicide rather than continue living without her husband. (There is no corresponding institution of glorious suicide for the man whose wife died; Stein 1978:253-68; Nobel 1979).

Certain structures in a community may be focuses of male activity; others are nodes of women's activities. Ceremonial structures may be men-only locations. The kiva, among certin Pueblo Indians, was such a feature, and in West Africa the "tombe" was a gathering place for men on the outskirts of villages (Silberfein 1976). The mosque in Islam has always welcomed men more than women. For Islamic women there is the tomb of a revered saint (Mernissi 1977). In the cool darkness of the tomb, women could pray the saint would make life easier. In desert areas of the Arab world, women typically congregate at the village well, for water and for female fellowship. While each woman waits her turn, she chats with neighbors. It may be her only occasion in the day to leave the confines of the courtyard. So important is the social function of the well that when it is replaced with indoor taps, women often complain bitterly. Men avoid the well, and a man drawing water receives the snickers of passers-by. For men (and not for women), there is the village "cantina," a small shop where coffee, tea, and soft drinks are served (the cantina is not a tavern since alcohol is prohibited in Islam). Men drink coffee, tell stories, discuss politics, and often listen to the inevitable transistor radio owned by the shop keeper.

In the West, the cantina becomes the neighborhood tavern, or perhaps the more elaborate institution, the men's club. Some such institutions have house rules making them totally segregated. Usually they are not, but women still prefer to avoid them unless escorted by a male (Fox 1977:814; Gorden *et al.:* Table 4). Until recently, Canada had a strange law requiring that taverns should have two separate sections, reached by separate doors, one clearly marked "men's entrance," the other "ladies and escorts." Apparently the male-only section was considered too crude and vulgar a place for proper women.

Unescorted women who are less than "proper" can be found in certain types of taverns, however; bar girls hustling drinks, dancers working the crowd when not on stage, and, of course, prostitutes — these women are welcome if they will provide easy friendship for a price. Establishments where sex is sold (brothels and less "hard core" places such as x-rated theaters and adult book-stores) impart a notorious identity to a landscape. Sometimes the establishments are well marked with overtly sexual material clearly in view; sometimes the clues are subtle. In Frankfurt, West Germany, the signs are blatant and unambiguous. The "combat zone," as the district is called, occupies many blocks. Virtually every establishment is identifiable as a place catering to the desires of men: brightly lit bars, pinball and videogame parlors, sexual paraphernalia shops, strip joints, x-rated movies, and hotels housing prostitutes. Brothels dominated the landscape of large areas of San Francisco during gold rush times *(Figure 21; Atlas of California* 1980). Although most are now gone, the Barbary Coast district, a short walk from Chinatown, is alive with flashing neon signs advertising nude dancing. In some cities prostitutes remain within brothels and beckon prospective clients through large windows on the street. Sometimes (more in the past than today) a red light over the door signals the presence of a brothel, hence the term, red light district. In New York City, brothels, as such, are not common; rather prostitutes walk the streets, taking clients to automobiles or hotels (Cohen 1980:106). In Nevada, the only U.S. state

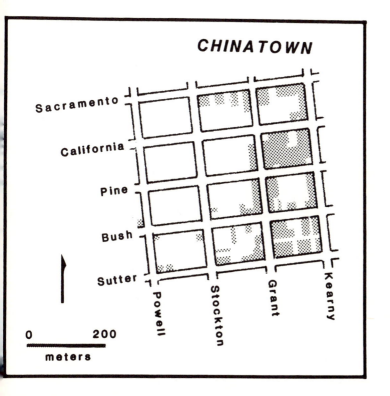

FIGURE 21   DOWNTOWN SAN FRANCISCO, 1887.
Shaded areas show the locations of brothels (after *Atlas of California* 1980: 22).

where prostitution is legalized, brothels are generally located in small towns (the counties containing Reno and Las Vegas prohibit prostitution). Consequently, cients usually drive to the brothels. The wealthy may fly to the houses' private air strips. The visual impact of brothel prostitution on the Nevada landscape is small, however, Brothels are usually clustered together on the "wrong side" of the railroad tracks. In order to present an inoffensive image, the form of the brothel generally belies its function. Except for the very poorest, it presents the clean facade of a middle class motel or bar. Their names may be somewhat suggestive ("Cottontail Ranch," "Valley of Love," "Players Club") but most houses could be mistaken as something else; advertising on the street or highway is prohibited. Consequently, the prospective client, receiving ambiguous clues from the environment, must request directions from locals (Symanski 1981; Symanski 1974; Rubin 1975).

Prostitution is illegal throughout most of the United States, but nude dancing and adult theaters and bookstores are not. In some communities the visual impact of such establishments is great. Strangers driving through a town with a large military base in the area recognize an unusually large collection of adult entertainment parlors. Elsewhere, they may be fewer in number and the facades more discreet; notwithstanding, their presence is offensive to many, and many communities would like them removed. However, in a New Jersey test case, the U.S. Supreme Court ruled that nude dancing is a form of expression protected by the First Amendment. Thus, the court protected nude dancing spots from being completely zoned out of a commercial area (*Time* 1981:56-7).

These places, where a women's value is a function only of her body and no other qualities matter, are locations of sexual exploitation in a community. Men depersonalize women in such establishments, making them into powerless, harmless objects which can be manipulated and toyed with. As such, they are blemishes on the face of the land (Stockard and Johnson 1980:243-45).

There are numerous other types of establishments — less vulgar to be sure — whose form reflects that they cater to men: for example, gun shops, auto supply stores, and auto body shops. Certainly the functions of these establishments reveal the clientele they wish to attract. So too does their form. From inside or outside, they present a masculine appearance: the features in the shops are rough-edged rather than delicate; the walls are plain rather than ornate; the signs are lettered with bold characters rather than cursive script. These are some of the numerous clues which suggest the gender of the shop's clientele.

Some shops cater to women. A male geography student recorded interesting personal observations investigating beauty parlors, bridal shops, maternity wear shops, and other establishments of the female domain. He was aware of delicate decorative embellishments, soft colors, inoffensive music, and distinct feminine scents. The growing trend toward unisex styling and gender role reversal allows many modern shops to communicate an androgynous message of universal appeal. However most shops which cater to one sex or the other still present unambiguous gender clues to their customers.

Her Landscape

An analysis of the impact of women on the cultural landscape reveals that many observable features of everyday life owe their existence and their specific form to the behavior patterns of women or to society's attitudes toward women. The gender-related landscape features are an odd collection: dress shops, topless bars, *sati* shines, menstruation rooms, Virgin Mary statues, Arab courtyard houses, and so forth. Many features are unhappy reminders of the essentially sexist nature of contemporary society. They are manifestations of what many feminists believe is an underlying universal hostility which men feel toward women.

Looking at the totality of the cultural landscape, one is impressed with the rich variety of human-created forms which are found on the land. Many of these objects are unrelated to gender; the list of those which are related to women is surprisingly small considering that women are more than half the population. Agriculture, industry, and urban design are dominated by men, and the landscapes associated with these activities owe their overall composition to the decisions made by men. One can only wonder how the landscape might appear in an egalitarian society. Unquestionably many (probably most) of the forms would be unchanged: the design of a steel-girder bridge, we assume, would be identical irrespective of the sex of the designer. The discriminatory and repressive institutions referenced above, and their landscape manifestations, would surely vanish from a landscape of egalitarian design. Other than that, what would be the form of an egalitarian landscape? The answer can only be imagined.

5

Her Space, Her Place

This book has been a geographer's view of the world of women, a brief atlas of woman's space and place. We now change the perspective and consider what women who are not geographers might observe in the world of academic geography.

Geographical methodology, with its emphasis on place and location, permits examination of feminist issues from unique perspectives. Geographical inquiry brings into sharp focus the consequences of the spatial propinquity of women and men, a propinquity shared by no other human groups. Few communities of any significant size are exclusively female or male. Although sex ratio may be balanced, the opportunities and achievements of women and men differ greatly. Employment patterns, educational levels, rights, and status are among many of the topics which vary between the sexes and vary from place to place. Statistics world-wide usually show that where differences exist between women and men according to some variable, women are disadvantaged. Based on standard socio-economic measures, it seems that the world of women is a depressed region.

The travel habits of women and men reveal sex selective patterns, both in terms of long-term migrations and short-term, day-to-day travel. Generally men travel farther away, more often, and to different places than women. Such is the consequence of the division of labor found in virtually all societies. Women clearly enjoy travel, perhaps as much as or more than men. However, because they suffer (or assume they suffer) excessively from physical disadvantages, travel for women without male companions is exceptional. The routes of travel in the world of women are familiar and well-worn paths leading out from the home.

Not surprisingly, the landscape contains tangible artifacts identifying places which are associated with one sex or the other. Sadly, however, when landscape features are linked with women, they often remind us of some inegalitarian institutions of society. Where, feminists ask, are the shrines and monuments honoring the glorious deeds of real, historical females? They are few indeed: "Only six of America's 200 historic sites and more than 2,000 landmarks commemorate women — and most of those have been established only in the past five years" (Moynehan 1980:26). One place which recently became enshrined to honor women (specifically, 19th century women who fought for equality) is Seneca Falls, New York. There, the meeting halls and houses where the suffrage movements began became in December, 1980, a national historic park dedicated to feminist courage (*Feminist Studies* 1980:412; Moynehan 1980:26).

For the most part, however, monuments on the landscape glorify the deeds of men. Mount Rushmore is one example, perhaps the most overwhelming one, but across the map there are thousands of smaller monuments honoring male personages. Similarly, everyday artifacts such as buildings and bridges owe their existence and form to the decisions and activities of men. Journeys through the world of women crisscross landscapes designed by men.

The science of geography rests on a millennia-old tradition of exploration. Studies of the alternate worlds of women and men, a few of which have been cited in this book, are explorations into new environments whose details reveal fascinating patterns of spatial order.

An inspection of academic geography might also reveal that what geographers say, and particularly how they say it, shows a lack of awareness of changes which are taking place in language. More and more writers now use "he or she" where formerly the masculine pronoun alone might have been used and for the generic 'man,' 'human' is now employed. Mention above was made of language in geographical texts such as the book *Man's Role in Changing the Face of the Earth*. Other books and authors could be cited as well which show little awareness of the language issue. Spencer and Thomas (1969:164), for example, might not have employed the many references to 'man' or the masculine pronoun in their description of paleolithic society if their book was written in the 1980s:

> Paleolithic **man** began early to express **his** curiosity about the nature of the physical materials around **him** on the surface of the earth. . . . **His** earliest knowledge [of the environment] was very limited, but **he** kept trying because **he** was **man** and **his** mind was stimulated and never satisfied (emphasis ours).

Hart (1975:172) might reword his description of a secretary, whom he calls "a sweet young thing in a miniskirt chewing gum and pounding a typewriter." The matter of language is receiving attention in geography and insensitivity to offensive wording can no longer be ignored. Studies reveal many examples such as those provided here where changes in wording could provide a more positive image of women (Larimore 1978).

Further investigation of academic geography would also reveal that women as professional geographers generally have had a less rewarding experience than men. Geography as a profession has been dominated by men, overwhelmingly so. In the first seventy-nine years of the Association of American Geographers, only one woman was elected President, Ellen Churchill Semple in 1921. The profession is attempting to put right the wrongs of the past, to be sure, and in recent years women geographers have been influential in the A.A.G. Many have held important leadership roles. For example, from 1950 to 1960 only 3 percent of the Association officers were women. But from 1970 to 1980 the figure had risen to 19 percent. The A.A.G. has committees for the study of the geographical perspectives on women and on the status of women in geography. The National Council for Geographic Education has similar committees, as do state and regional geography groups. Today women interested in professional geography can be assured that the profession welcomes productive scholars and teachers, women and men alike.

The nature of geography, as graduate students quickly learn, changes constantly. This book may have revealed dimensions of the field which previously went unnoticed or were given little attention. Many themes may, at first glance, seem mundane, trivial, and inappropriate for serious geographical study. The matter of housework, for example, might appear so. Yet housework and the role of the homemaker are research themes treated with great seriousness in other disciplines. No less a scholar than economist John K. Galbraith (1974) has written on the subject: *The Sociology of Housework* is an often-quoted work (Oakley 1974; Mainardi 1970).

Likewise the matters of love, romance, sexual passion are themes rarely encountered in geographical literature. These issues are serious matters of study in other disciplines, however, and no one will deny the interest they hold for the population as a whole. They are presented here in a geographical context because they are a natural and logical result of scholarship in which the population is disaggregated on the basis of sex. Moreover, these themes are discussed because they reveal formerly unknown aspects of human spatial organizations

Many topics have been omitted or given only cursory treatment; this book is intended to reveal major features and cannot explore all the areas in the depth they deserve. Women on the frontier could have been discussed — how their perceptual and behavioral patterns differed from those of men. Women in the ecology movement is a subject worthy of examination — some ecology activists contend that women have been more sensitive to the earth and its problems than men. Since geographers have long been interested in the stewardship of the earth and attitudes toward resources, they would welcome scholarship of this type. Numerous studies of patterns of spatial distributions and spatial movements could be done, and case studies of women in particular societies would be valuable, Sweden compared with Spain, for example, or the United States with the Soviet Union.

Clearly there are multitudes of spatial patterns in the world of women awaiting discovery. The geographical exploration of women's place and space has produced, thus far, only a sketch map of the periphery.

Bibliography

Abadan-Unat, N. 1977. "Implications of Migration on Emancipation and Pseudo-emancipation of Turkish Women," *International Migration Review* 11:31-57.

Abler, R. et al. 1971. *Spatial Organization, The Geographer's View of the World.* Englewood Cliffs, NJ: Prentice-Hall, Inc.

Ahmed, L. 1982. "Western Ethnocentrism and Perception of the Harem," *Feminist Studies* 8:521-34.

Anderson, J. and M. Tindall. 1972. "The Concept of Home Range: New Data for the Study of Territorial Behavior," pp. 111-117 in W.J. Mitchell (editor), *Environmental Design: Research and Practice* (Proceedings of the EDRA Conference, University of California, Los Angeles).

Andrews, A. 1982. "Towards a Status-of-Women Index," *The Professional Geographer* 34:24-31.

Arnett, R. J. 1975. *Female and Male Images in the Built Environment: A Study of Dominant Cultural Images in Architecture and Women Architects in Oregon.* Unpublished Master of Architecture thesis, Department of Architecture, University of Oregon.

Atlas of California. 1980. Portland, OR: The Book Broker.

Badinter, E. 1981. *Mother Love, Myth and Reality, Motherhood in Modern History.* New York: Macmillan.

Barry, K. 1979. *Female Sexual Slavery.* Englewood Cliffs, NJ: Prentice-Hall.

Beard, W. 1978. *"Rape in Tallahassee: A Cartographic Analysis of Some Demographic, Environmental, Socio-Economic, and Temporal Factors.* Unpublished M.A. thesis, Department of Geography, Florida State University.

Beguin, J.-P. et al. 1952. *L'habitat au Cameroun.* Paris: Publication de l'Office de la Recherche Scientifique Outre Mer et Editions de l'Union Française.

Bernard, C. and E. Schlaffer. 1981. "The Man in the Street: Why He Harasses," *Ms. Magazine* 1981 (May):18.

Birdsall, S. S. and J. M. Gunville. 1976. "Numerical Sex Imbalance in Washington, D.C., 1940-70." Paper presented at the annual meeting of the Association of American Geographers, New York.

Blumenthal, W. H. 1962. *Brides From Bridewell: Female Felons Sent to Colonial America.* Westport, CT: Greenwood Press.

Bollet, J. 1981. "A Window on ¾ of the World," *Ms. Magazine* 1981 (March):20.

Boserup, E. 1970. *Women's Role in Economic Development.* London: Allen and Unwin.

Boutelle, S. 1977. "Julia Morgan," pp. 79-87 in S. Torre (editor), *Women in American Architecture: A Historic and Contemporary Perspective.* New York: Whitney Library of Design, Watson-Guptill Publishers.

Bowlby, S. R. et al. 1981. "Feminism and Geography," *Area* 13:19-25.

Broek, J. O. and J. W. Webb. 1978. *A Geography of Mankind,* 3rd ed. New York: McGraw-Hill.

Broward County Human Relations Division, Women's Concerns Section. 1978. *Profile Broward Women.* Ft. Lauderdale, Broward County, Florida.

Brown, B. et al. 1977. *Women's Rights and the Law: The Impact of the ERA on State Laws.* New York: Praeger Publishers.

Brown, L. A. et al. 1972. *Day Care Centers in Columbus: A Locational Strategy.* Columbus, Ohio: Department of Geography, Ohio State University, Discussion Paper 26.

Brown, L. A. et al. 1974. "The Location of Urban Population Service Facilities: A Strategy and Its Application," *Social Science Quarterly* 54, 4:784-99.

Bruegel, I. 1973. "Cities, Women and Social Class: A Comment," *Antipode: A Radical Journal of Geography* 5, 3:62-3.

Burnett, P. 1973. "Social Change, The Status of Women and Models of City Form and Development," *Antipode: A Radical Journal of Geography* 5, 3:57-62.

Burton, L. 1976. "The Country and the City: The Effects of Women's Changing Roles and Attitudes on their Views of the Environment in Contemporary Fiction." Unpublished paper.

Carter, G. F. 1964. *Man and the Land, A Cultural Geography.* New York: Holt, Rinehart and Winston.

Cichocki, M. K. 1980. "Women's Travel Patterns in a Suburban Development," pp. 151-164 in G. R. Wekerle *et al.* (editors), *New Space for Women.* Boulder, CO: Westview Press.

Clarke, J. I. 1970. "Population Distribution and Dynamics in Cameroon," in W. Zelinsky *et al.* (editors), *Geography and a Crowding World.* New York: Oxford University Press.

Cohen, B. 1980. *Deviant Street Networks.* Lexington, MA: D.C. Heath.

Cole, D. 1973. *From Tipi to Skyscraper: A History of Women in Architecture.* Boston: I Press.

Curtis, J. R. 1980. "Miami's Little Havana: Yard Shrines, Cult Religion and Landscape," *Journal of Cultural Geography* 1:1-15.

Devereux, G. 1967. "A Typological Study of Abortion in 350 Primitive, Ancient, and Pre-Industrial Societies," pp. 97-152 in H. Rosen (editor), *Abortion in America.* Boston: Beacon Press.

Dillard, A. 1974. *Pilgrim at Tinker Creek.* New York: Harper Magazine Press (Harper and Row).

Dowling, C. 1981. *The Cinderella Complex. Women's Hidden Fear of Independence.* New York: Summit Books.

Dreifus, C. 1980. "Tactics for Traveling Alone," *Ms. Magazine* 1980 (August):94-5.

Early, J. 1980. Private communication.

Eby, S. M. 1979. "The Swords Started Out as Plowshares," *Ms. Magazine* 1979 (August):23.

Epstein, C. F. 1970. *Woman's Place.* Berkeley and Los Angeles: University of California Press.

Ericksen, J. 1977. "An Analysis of the Journey to Work for Women," *Social Problems* 24:428-35.

Erwin, N. 1978. "Regional Variation in the Legal Rights of Women." Paper presented at the annual meeting of the Southeastern Division of the Association of American Geographers, Athens, Georgia.

Everitt, J. C. 1976. "Community and Propinquity in a City," *Annals, Association of American Geographers* 66:104-16.

Fagnani, J. 1977. "Activités Féminines et Transports Urbains," *Annales de Géographie* 86:542-61.

Faragher, J. M. 1979. *Women and Men on the Oregon Trail.* New Haven, CT: Yale University Press.

Farnsworth, J. 1980. "Networks," *Transition, Quarterly Journal of the Socially and Ecologically Responsible Geographers* 10, 2:23-25.

Farrell, W. 1975. *The Liberated Man.* New York: Bantam Books.

Fava, S. F. 1980. "Women's Place in the New Suburbia," pp. 97-152 in G.R. Wekerle *et al.* (editors), *New Space for Women.* Boulder: Westview Press.

Feminist Studies. 1980. "Women's Rights National Park in Seneca Falls," *Feminist Studies* 6:412.

Fisher, E. 1979. *Woman's Creation: Sexual Evolution and the Shaping of Society.* Garden City, NY: Anchor Press/Doubleday.

Fowles, J. 1980. *Islands.* Boston: Little, Brown and Co.

Fox, L. G. 1977. " 'Nice Girl': Social Control of Women Through a Value Construct," *Signs: Journal of Women in Culture and Society* 2, 4:805-17.

Freestone, R. 1977. "Provision of Child Care Facilities in Sydney," *The Australian Geographer* 13:318-25.

Friedan, B. 1963. *The Feminine Mystique.* New York: Norton.

Friedl, E. 1975. *Women and Men: An Anthropologist's View.* New York: Holt, Rinehart and Winston.

Fuller, G. A. 1973. "Diffusion of Illegal Abortion in Santiago De Chile: The Use of a Direction-Bias Model," *Proceedings of the Association of American Geographers* 5:71-4

Fuller, G. *et al.* 1980. "Areal Fertility in Sri Lanka." Presented at the annual meeting of the Association of American Geographers, Louisville.

Galbraith, J. K. 1974. "How the Economy Hangs on Her Apron Strings," *Ms. Magazine* 1974 (May):74-77

Galland, C. 1980. *Women in the Wilderness.* New York: Harper Colophon Books.

Gellis, A. N. 1981. *An Analysis of the Geography of Sex Ratio in the United States.* Unpublished M.A. thesis, Department of Geography, Florida Atlantic University.

Glazer-Malbin, N. 1976. "Housework," *Signs: Journal of Women in Culture and Society* 1,4:905-22

Gordon, M. T. *et al.* 1980. "Crime, Women, and the Quality of Urban Life," *Signs: Journal of Women in Culture and Society* 5,3:S144-S160.

Gosal, G. S. and G. Krishan. 1975. "Patterns of Internal Migration in India," pp. 193-206 in L.A. Kosinski and R.M. Prothero (editors), *People on the Move, Studies on Internal Migration.* London: Methuen.

Gould, P. R. 1969. *Spatial Diffusion.* Washington, DC: Association of American Geographers, Commission on College Geography, Resource Paper 4.

Green, D. B. 1977. "The Marriage Field of a Rural Mountain Valley in the Mormon Culture Region." Presented at the annual meeting of the Association of American Geographers, Salt Lake City.

Grover, S. 1980. "The Bodice-Busters: A Sure-Fire Formula for Literary Success," *Wall Street Journal,* November 5, 1980:1,28.

Guiliano, G. 1979. "Public Transportation and the Travel Means of Women," *Traffic Quarterly* 33:606-16.

Haglund, D. K. 1969. "The Population of Northern North America," pp. 271-90 in P.F. Griffin (editor), *Geography of Population, A Teacher's Guide.* Palo Alto, CA: Fearon Publishers.

Harries, K. D. 1974. *The Geography of Crime and Justice.* New York: McGraw-Hill.

Harris, L. J. 1978. "Sex Differences in Spatial Ability: Possible Environmental, Genetic, and Neurological Factors," pp. 405-522 in M. Kinsbourne (editor) *Asymmetrical Function of the Brain.* Cambridge: Cambridge University Press.

Harris, L. J. 1979. "Sex-Related Differences in Spatial Ability: A Developmental Psychological View," pp. 133-81 in C. B. Kopp (editor) *Becoming Female, Perspectives on Development.* New York: Plenum Press.

Harris, M. 1978. *Cows, Pigs, Wars and Witches, The Riddles of Culture.* New York: Vintage Books.

Harrison, H. S. 1973. *Houses. The Illustrated Guide to Construction, Designs, and Systems.* Chicago: National Association of Real Estate Brokers.

Hart, J. F. 1975. *The Look of the Land.* Englewood Cliffs, NJ: Prentice-Hall.

Hayden, D. 1977. "Catharine Beecher and the Politics of Housework," pp. 40-49 in S. Torre (editor), *Women in American Architecture: A Historic and Contemporary Perspective.* New York: Whitney Library of Design and Watson-Guptill Publishers.

Hayden, D. 1978. "Two Utopian Feminists and Their Campaigns for Kitchenless Houses," *Signs: Journal of Women in Culture and Society* 4, 2:274-90.

Hayden, D. 1980a. "Redesigning the Domestic Workplace," pp. 101-121 in G. R. Wekerle *et al.* (editors), *New Space for Women.* Boulder, CO: Westview Press.

Hayden, D. 1980b. "What Would a Non-Sexist City Be Like? Speculations on Housing, Urban Design, and Human Work," *Signs: Journal of Women in Culture and Society* 5,3:S170-S187.

Hayghe, H. 1974. "Marital and Family Characteristics of the Labor Force in March 1973," *Monthly Labor Review* 97:21-27,

Heide, W. S. 1973. "Keynote Address," *NOW Acts, Proceedings of the Sixth National Conference of the National Organization of Women,* 6,1:2-7

Hennessee, J. A. 1981. "Progress: Hotels, Airlines, and Even Bartenders Are Catering to Businesswomen," *Ms. Magazine* 1981 (February):38-41.

Henry, N. F. 1979. "Abortion Facilities in the Northeastern United States: Diffusion Barriers and Shifts in Patterns." Presented at the annual meeting of the Association of American Geographers, Philadelphia.

Hirt, H. F. 1978. "Caste and House Type in South India." Paper presented at the annual meeting of the Association of American Geographers, New Orleans.

Hoffman, L. W. 1974. "The Employment of Women, Education, and Fertility," *Merrill-Palmer Quarterly* 20:99-120.

Holcomb, B. and B. Parkoff. 1980. "Sex Differences in the Role of the Home Place Among the Elderly." Presented at the annual meeting of the Association of American Geographers, Louisville.

Holmes, J. et al. 1972. "Facility Location Under a Maximum Travel Restriction: An Example Using Day Care Facilities," *Geographical Analysis* 4:258-66.

Huntington, E. 1959. *Mainsprings of Civilization.* New York: Mentor Books.

International Labor Organization, Office for Women. 1981. "Women, Technology and the Development Process," pp. 33-47 in R. Dauber and M.L. Cain (editors), *Women and Technological Change in Development Countries.* Boulder, CO: Westview Press for the American Association for the Advancement of Science.

Jacobs, K. L. 1980. "Celia Thaxter and Her Island Garden," *Landscape* 24, 3:12-17.

James, N. 1979. "Naomi James: An Amazing Lone Journey," National Public Radio Cassettes, No. HO-79-12-12.

Johnson, A. G. 1980. "On the Prevalence of Rape in the United States," *Signs: Journal of Women in Culture and Society* 6,1:136-46.

Joyce, T. A. 1908. *Women of All Nations: A Record of Their Characteristics, Habits, Manners, Customs and Influence.* London: Cassell and Company, Ltd.

Kadushin, A. 1980. *Child Welfare Services.* New York: Macmillan.

Kelly, C. 1977. *Marriage Migration in Massachusetts, 1765-1790.* Syracuse, NY: Department of Geography, Syracuse University, Discussion Paper 30.

Klimasewski, T. 1974. "Spatial Variations in Women's Share of the Manufacturing Labor Force in Tennessee: A Statistical Analysis," *Geographical Bulletin* 11:40-46.

LaBastille, A. 1980. *Women and Wilderness; Women in Wilderness Professions and Lifestyle.* San Francisco: Sierra Club Books.

Larimore, A. E. 1978. "Humanizing the Writing in Cultural Geography Textbooks," *Journal of Geography* 77:183-85.

Lee, D. 1967. "The Geography of Rural House Types in the Nile Valley of Northern Sudan." Unpublished Ph.D. dissertation, Department of Geography, University of California, Los Angeles.

Lee, D. et al. 1979. "The Geography of Female Status: A World-Wide View," *Transition, Quarterly Journal of the Socially and Ecologically Responsible Geographers* 9,2:2-7

Lee, D. and B. Loyd. 1982. *Women and Geography: A Bibliography.* Cincinnati: University of Cincinnati, Society of the Socially and Ecologically Responsible Geographers.

Lee, D. and R. Schultz, 1982. "Regional Patterns of Female Status in the United States," *The Professional Geographer,* 34:32-41.

Leo, J. 1980. "Down with Motherhood," *Time,* July 28, 1980:78.

Libbee, M. J. and D. E. Sopher. 1975. "Marriage Migration in Rural India," p. 347-60 in L. A. Kosinski and R. M. Prothero (editors), *People on the Move. Studies on Internal Migration.* London: Methuen and Co.

Liverman, D. M. and D. J. Sherman. 1981. "The Disaster Novel," Paper presented at the annual meeting of the Association of American Geographers, Los Angeles.

Lorber, J. et al. 1981. "On *The Reproduction of Mothering:* A Methodological Debate," *Signs: Journal of Women in Culture and Society* 6:482-514.

Loyd, B. 1973. "Male and Female Differences in Spatial Mobility," *Proceedings of the Middle States Division, Association of American Geographers* 3:23-25.

Loyd, B. 1977. "Community in California," *California Geographer* 17:73-81

Loyd, B. 1982. "Women, Home and Status," pp. 181-97 in J. Duncan (editor), *Housing and Identity.* New York: Holmes and Meier.

Loyd, B. and L. Rowntree. 1978. "Radical Feminists and Gay Men in San Francisco: Social Space in Dispersed Communities," pp. 78-88 in D. Lanegran and R. Palm (editors), *Invitation to Geography.* New York: McGraw-Hill.

Madden, J. F. 1977. "A Spatial Theory of Sex Discrimination," *Journal of Regional Science* 17,3:369-80.

Mainardi, R. 1970. *Politics of Housework.* Pittsburgh: Know, Inc.

Markusen, A. R. 1981. "City Spatial Structure, Women's Household Work, and National Urban Policy," in C. R. Simpson *et al.* (editors), *Women and the American City.* Chicago: Chicago Press.

Mayfield, R. C. 1972. "The Spatial Structure of a Selected Interpersonal Contact: A Regional Comparison of Marriage Distances In India," pp. 385-401 in P. W. English and R. C. Mayfield (editors), *Man, Space, and Environment, Concepts in Contemporary Human Geography.* New York: Oxford University Press.

Mazey, M. E. and T. Seiler. No date. "Women in Suburbia." Unpublished manuscript.

McCullough, J. 1973. "The 13 Who Were Left Behind," *Ms. Magazine* 1973 (September): 41-45.

Mead, M. 1976. "A Comment on the Role of Women in Agriculture," pp. 9-11 in I. Tinker and M. Bramsen (editors), *Women and World Development.* Washington, DC: Overseas Development Council for the American Association for the Advancement of Science.

Mead, M. 1981. "The Glass Boot Syndrome. Review of *The Cinderella Complex: Women's Hidden Fear of Independence* by Collette Dowling," *Ms. Magazine* 1981 (April):34-35.

Mercier, P. 1954. "L'Habitation à Étage dans l'Atakora," *Études Dahoméennes* 11:30-78.

Mernissi, F. 1977. "Women, Saints, and Sanctuaries," *Signs: Journal of Women in Culture and Society* 3,1:101-112.

Meyer, J. W. 1975. "Diffusion of an American Montessori Education." Chicago, IL: Department of Geography, University of Chicago, Research Paper 160.

Monk, J. 1981. "Social Change and Sexual Differences in Puerto Rican Rural Migration," pp. 28-43 in O.H. Horst (editor), *Papers in Latin American Geography in Honor of Lucia C. Harrison.* Muncie, IN: Conference of Latin Americanist Geographers.

Monk, J. and A. Rengert. 1982. "Locational Decision Making: The Case of the Day Care Center," pp. 11-24 in A. Rengert and J. Monk 1982a.

Monmonier, M. S. and A. V. Williams. 1973. "Abortion and Spatial Interaction: Temporary Migration to New York," *Proceedings of the Association of American Geographers* 5:177-80.

Morley, D. 1980. "Introduction to Women in Environmental Decision-making: Institutional Constraints," pp. 201-204 in G. R. Wekerle *et al.* (editors), *New Space for Women.* Boulder, CO: Westview Press.

Moynehan, B. 1980. "Seneca Falls Rises: From Laundromat to Women's Rights National Park," *Ms. Magazine* 1980 (January):26.

***Ms. Magazine.* 1977.** "Women Design Space," *Ms. Magazine* 1977 (March):63-67.

Munroe, R. L. and R. H. Munroe. 1971. "Effect of Environmental Experience on Spatial Ability in an East African Society," *Journal of Social Psychology* 83,1:15-22.

Noble, W.A. 1979. "Sati (Wife Suicide) in India." Paper delivered at the annual meeting of the Association of American Geographers, Philadelphia.

Oakley, A. 1974. *The Sociology of Housework.* New York: Pantheon Books.

Ohio Department of Economic and Community Development. 1973. *Model Zoning Regulations,* 2nd. ed. Columbus.

Oshiro, K. 1978. "Female Seasonal Migration from Rural Areas of Japan," *East Lakes Geographer* 13:45-61.

Oshiro, K. 1982. Private communication.

Paine, J. 1977. "Pioneer Women Architects," pp. 54-69 in S. Torre (editor), *Women in American Architecture: A Historic and Contemporary Perspective.* New York: Whitney Library of Design and Watson-Guptill Publishers.

Palm, R. 1979. "The Daily Activities of Women," in E. Moen *et al. (editors), Women and Energy Development: Impact and Resource.* Boulder, CO: University of Colorado.

Palm, R. and A. Pred. 1974. *A Time-Geographic Perspective on Problems of Inequality for Women.* Berkeley: University of California, Institute of Urban and Regional Development, Working Paper 236.

Palm, R. and A. Pred. 1978. "The Status of American Women: A Time Geographic View," pp. 99-109 in D. Lanegran and R. Palm (editors), *An Invitation to Geography.* New York: McGraw-Hill.

Parlee, M. B. 1975. "Psychology," *Signs: Journal of Women in Culture and Society* 1,1:119-38.

***People* 1978.** "Abortion," *People* 5,2:4-21.

Perpillou, A. V. 1966. *Human Geography.* New York: John Wiley and Sons.

Perry, P. J. 1969. "Working-Class Isolation and Mobility in Rural Dorset, 1837-1936: A Study of Marriage Distances," *Transactions, Institute of British Geographers* 49:121-140.

Peters, G. L. 1976. "The Sex Selectivity of Out-Migration: An Appalachian Example." *Yearbook, Association of Pacific Coast Geographers* 38:99-109.

Population Crisis Committee. 1979. "World Abortion Trends," *Population* 9 (April):1-6.

Pochoda, E. 1979. "Garden-Variety Art," *Ms. Magazine* 1979 (November):45.

Popenoe, D. 1980. "Women in the Suburban Environment: A U.S.-Sweden Comparison," pp. 165-74. in G. R. Wekerle *et al.* (editors), *New Space for Women.* Boulder, CO: Westview Press.

Porteous, J. D. 1976. "Home: The Territorial Core," *Geographical Review* 66:383-90.

Prussin, L. 1969. *Architecture in Northern Ghana, A Study of Forms and Functions.* Berkeley and Los Angeles: University of California Press.

Prussin, L. 1972. "West African Mud Granaries," *Paideuma, Mitteilungen zur Kulturkunde* 18:144-69.

Raglan, L. 1964. *The Temple and the House.* London: Routledge and Kegan Paul.

Rapoport, A. 1969. *House Form and Culture.* Englewood Cliffs, NJ: Prentice-Hall.

Rengert, A. 1981. "Some Sociocultural Aspects of Rural Out-Migration in Latin America," pp. 15-27 in O. H. Horst (editor), *Papers in Latin American Geography in Honor of Lucia C. Harrison.* Muncie, IN: Conference of Latin Americanist Geographers.

Rengert, A. and J. Monk (editors). 1982a. *Women and Spatial Change: Learning Resources for Social Science Courses.* Dubuque, IA: Kendall/Hunt.

Rengert, A. and J. Monk. 1982b. "Village to Barriada: Contemporary Female Migration to Cities in Latin America," pp. 25-28 in A. Rengert and J. Monk 1982a.

Rengert, G. 1975. "Some Effects of Being Female on Criminal Spatial Behavior," *The Pennsylvania Geographer* 13, 3:10-18.

Rengert, G. and J. Monk. 1982. "Geographic Perspectives on Social Change: The Example of Women in Crime," pp. 5-10 in A. Rengert and J. Monk 1982a.

Rimbert, S. and T. Vogt. 1978. "Innovation et Aires de Comportement: La Contraception en Alsace." *L'Espace Géographique* 4:271-77.

Robinson, J. P. 1977. *How Americans Use Time.* New York: Praeger.

Rock, C. et al. 1980. "The Appropriation of the House: Changes in House Design and Concepts of Domesticity," pp.83-100 in G. R. Wekerle et al. (editors) *New Space for Women.* Boulder, CO: Westview Press.

Roder, W. 1977. "An Alternate Interpretation of Men and Women in Geography," *The Professional Geographer* 29:397-400.

Rossi, A. 1969. "The Beginning of Ideology: Alternate Models of Sex Equality," *The Humanist* 16:3-6.

Rothman, S. M. 1978. *Woman's Proper Place: A History of Changing Ideas and Practices, 1970 to the Present.* New York: Basic Books.

Rubenstein, C. 1980. "Survey Report: How Americans View Vacations," *Psychology Today* 1980 (May):62-76.

Rubin, B. 1975. "Commentary on 'Prostitution in Nevada'," *Annals, Association of American Geographers* 65:113-15.

Ryan, M. P. 1979. "The Power of Women's Networks: A Case Study of Female Moral Reform in Antebellum America," *Feminist Studies* 5,1:66-85

Saegert, S. 1980. "Masculine Cities and Feminine Suburbs." *Signs: Journal of Women in Culture and Society* 5,3:S96-S111.

Sauer, C. O. 1962. "Seashore — Primitive Home of Man?" *Proceedings, American Philosophical Society* 106:41-47.

Science News. 1976. Abortion Increasing Worldwide," *Science News* 1976 (March 13): 106.

Seymour, L. 1976. "Migration, Race, Sex and Class." Presented at the annual meeting of the Canadian Association of Geographers, Quebec City.

Shorter, E. 1977. "On Writing the History of Rape," *Signs: Journal of Women in Culture and Society* 3,2:471-82.

Silberfein, M. 1976. "Changing Circulation and Economic Activities among African Women." Unpublished manuscript.

Sklar, A. 1976. *Runaway Wives.* New York: Coward, McCann and Geoghegan.

Smith, H. 1977. *The Russians.* New York: Ballantine Books.

Sopher, D.E. 1979. "Sex Disparity in Indian Literacy," pp. 130-88 in D. Sopher (editor), *An Exploration of India.* Ithaca, NY: Cornell University Press.

Spencer, J. E. and W. Thomas. 1969. *Cultural Geography.* New York: John Wiley and Sons.

Spencer, R. F. et al. 1977. *The Native Americans.* New York: Harper and Row.

Stein, D. K. 1978. "Women to Burn: Suttee as a Normative Institution," *Signs: Journal of Women in Culture and Society* 4, 2:253-68.

Stockard, J. and M. M. Johnson. 1980. *Sex Roles; Sex Inequality and Sex Role Development.* Englewood Cliffs, NJ: Prentice-Hall, Inc.

Strobel, M. 1982. "African Women," *Signs: Journal of Women in Culture and Society,* 8:109-31.

Stutz, F. P. 1976. *Social Aspects of Interaction and Transportation.* Washington, DC: Association of American Geographers, Resource Papers for College Geography 76-2.

Sullivan, J. 1981. Quoted in *Time* 1981 (April 13):101.

Sweet, E. 1980. "Ms. Gazette: Summer Vacations, Resorts, Retreats, Tours, and Festivals," *Ms. Magazine* 1980 (May):79-82.

Symanski, R. 1974. "Prostitution in Nevada," *Annals, Association of American Geographers* 64:357-377.

Symanski, R. 1981. *The Immoral Landscape; Female Prostitution in Western Societies.* Toronto: Butterworths.

Tanner, N. M. 1981. *On Becoming Human.* New York: Cambridge University Press.

Tanner, N. and A. Zihlman. 1976. "Women in Evolution. Part 1: Innovation and Selection in Human Origins," *Signs: Journal of Women in Culture and Society* 1, 3, Part 1:585-608.

Taub, N. and G. O'Kane. 1981. "Women, The Family and Housing: Legal Trends," pp. 175-94 in Suzanne Keller (editor), *Building for Women.* Lexington, MA: Lexington Books.

Time. **1977a.** "The Unmaking of an Amendment." *Time* 1977 (April 25):89.

Time. **1977b.** "The Panic of Open Spaces; Overcoming the Terrors of Agoraphobia." *Time* 1977 (November 7):58.

Time. **1981.** "Incongruity at the High Court — A Mantle for Nude Dancing," *Time* 1981 (June 15):56-7.

Tinker, I. 1981. "New Technologies for Food-Related Activities: An Equity Strategy," pp. 51-88 in R. Dauber and M. L. Cain (editors), *Women and Technological Change in Developing Countries.* Boulder, CO: Westview Press for the American Association for the Advancement of Science.

Tivers, J. 1977. *Constraints on Spatial Activity Patterns: Women With Young Children.* London: Department of Geography, King's College, Occasional Paper 6.

Thomas, W. L., Jr. (editor). 1956. *Man's Role in Changing the Face of the Earth.* Chicago: University of Chicago Press.

Tognoli, J. 1979. "The Flight from Domestic Space: Men's Roles in the Household," *The Family Coordinator* 28:599-607.

Trewartha, G. 1969. *A Geography of Population: World Patterns.* New York: John Wiley and Sons.

Tuan, Y.-F. 1973. "Ambiguity in Attitudes Toward Environment," *Annals, Association of American Geographers* 63:411-23.

Tuan, Y.-F. 1974. *Topophilia; A Study of Environmental Perception, Attitudes, and Values.* Englewood Cliffs, NJ: Prentice-Hall.

United Nations. 1979. *Demographic Yearbook.* New York: United Nations.

U.S. Bureau of the Census. 1972. "Census of Population: 1970. State Economic Areas Final Report." Washington, DC: U.S. Government Printing Office.

U.S. Bureau of the Census. 1980a. *Statistical Abstract of the United States: 1980.* Washington, DC: U.S. Government Printing Office.

U.S. Bureau of the Census. 1980b. *A Statistical Portrait of Women in the United States: 1978.* Washington, DC: U.S. Government Printing Office.

U.S. Bureau of the Census. 1981. *1980 Census of Population, Supplementary Report PC80-S1-1.* Washington, DC: U.S. Government Printing Office.

Van Gelder, L. 1981. "The International Language of Street Hassling," *Ms. Magazine* 1981 (May):15-18.

Vaughter, R. M. 1976. "Psychology," *Signs: Journal of Women in Culture and Society,* 2, 1:120-46.

Wagner, P. L. 1972. *Environments and Peoples.* Englewood Cliffs, NJ: Prentice-Hall.

Waldman, E. and K. Gover. 1971. "Children of Women in the Labor Force," *Monthly Labor Review* 94 (July):19-25.

Washburne, C. K. and D. L. Chambless. 1978. "Afraid to Leave the House? You May Have Agoraphobia," *Ms. Magazine* 1978 (September):46-7.

Wekerle, G. R. et al. 1980. "Introduction," pp. 1-34 in G. R. Wekerle *et al.* (editors). *New Space for Women.* Boulder, CO: Westview Press.

Werner, K. 1980. "Swedish Women in Single-Family Housing," pp. 175-188 in G. R. Wekerle *et al.* (editors), *New Space for Women.* Boulder, CO: Westview Press.

Wheeler, J. O. and F. P. Stutz. 1971. "Spatial Dimensions of Urban Social Travel," *Annals, Association of American Geographers* 61:371-86.

Wilson, J. 1980. "News of Networking," Women's Educational Equality Communications 1980:1.

Wohl, L. C. 1982 "Rise in Antiabortion Terrorism," *Ms. Magazine* 1982 (November):19.

Wohlenberg, E. H. 1980. "Correlates of Equal Rights Amendment Ratification," *Social Science Quarterly* 60:676-84.

Women's Programme Unit, Human Resources Development Division, United Nations Economic Commission for Africa. 1975. "Africa's Food Producers: The Impact of Change on Rural Women," *Focus* (American Geographical Society) 25, 5:1-8.

Wright, J. K. 1947. "Terrae Incognitae, The Place of Imagination in Geography," *Annals, Association of American Geographers,* 37:1-15.

Wrightman, L. S. and K. Deaux. 1981. *Social Psychology in the '80s.* Monterrey, CA: Brooks/Cole.

Yacher, L. 1977. "Marriage Migration and Racial Mixing in Colonial Tlazazalca (Michoacan, Mexico), 1750-1800." Syracuse, NY: Department of Geography, Syracuse University, Discussion Paper 32.

Zelinsky, W. et al. 1982. "Women and Geography: A Review and Prospectus," *Progress in Human Geography* 6:317-66.

Zihlman, A. L. 1978. "Women in Evolution, Part II: Subsistence and Social Organization among Early Hominids," *Signs: Journal of Women in Culture and Society* 4, 1:4-20.